Staring at Lakes

Michael Harding is an author and playwright. His creative chronicle of ordinary life in the Irish midlands is published as a weekly column in *The Irish Times*. He has published three novels, *Priest*, *The Trouble with Sarah Gullion* and *Bird in the Snow*.

Staring at Lakes

A memoir of love, melancholy and magical thinking

MICHAEL HARDING

HACHETTE
BOOKS
IRELAND

First published in 2013 by Hachette Books Ireland

'The Donkey' by G.K. Chesterton used by permission of A P Watt Ltd, on behalf of the Royal Literary Fund.

Good Evening Mister Collins by Tom MacIntyre (*The Dazzling Dark: New Irish Plays*, London: Faber 1996) used by permission of the author

Through the Looking Glass, and What Alice Found There by Lewis Carroll (1871).

Some of the names and details in this book have been changed to protect the identity of individuals.

A CIP catalogue record for this title is available from the British Library.

ISBN 978 144474349 4

Typeset in AGaramond and MrsEaves by Bookends Publishing Services
Printed and bound by CPI Group (UK) Ltd, Croydon, CR0 4YY

Hachette Books Ireland policy is to use papers that are natural, renewable and recyclable products and made from wood grown in sustainable forests. The logging and manufacturing processes are expected to conform to the environmental regulations of the country of origin.

Hachette Books Ireland
8 Castlecourt Centre, Castleknock, Dublin 15, Ireland

A division of Hachette UK Ltd
338 Euston Road, London NW1 3BH
www.hachette.ie

For Sophia, with love

Part One
You can't go on forever

I can hear the porridge coming. It's on the stairs. I can hear it rattling on her tray as she climbs up to the landing. And now she's outside. She must put the tray on the floor to open the door.

But who is this with the porridge? Who have we here, this woman carrying my tray? She's not used to trays. She is uncertain with a tray.

'Shall I open the curtains?' she asks.

'No,' I say. 'No. Please don't. I can't bear the summer sun.'

3

But she opens them ever so slightly, so she can see her way around the bed.

She leaves me the porridge with honey and the omelette and toast and the mug of tea, leaves it on the bed, beside my legs. And then she goes away. I'm still in the dark, though I can just make out the food on the tray. When she's gone, I eat, gently, hoping nothing damages my stomach. And when all the food is gone, I place the tray on the floor beside the door, and I close the curtains.

It's the second day of June 2011. I am in the bedroom of Shandonagh House, an elegant nineteenth-century building on the outskirts of Mullingar. It's a long time since I left Leitrim.

My therapist says that there is something divided in each of us. And I agree. There are two parts; at least there is in me. For example, I am walking on a beach and I like what I am doing. It's beautiful. But inside me a contrary part doesn't connect. I like the wind and the surf, but the contrary part won't engage. Refuses to participate in the 'now'. A dark brooding shadow within watches me with indifference, or wants to wander in the past, along the laneways of regret and remorse. That is depression.

I thought marriage might protect me from depression. Marriage is a happy thing. It's something you do in a white dress and a morning suit, with family and friends in a beautiful hotel. She, especially she, looks radiant. Like a swan or a princess dressed up in magnolia ruffles that make the wedding guests dizzy thinking about where you might unfold her, open her and enter her.

That wasn't quite what we did or thought. The artist and me. We were both forty. She had been married and divorced already and her son was a big man of twenty-one standing at the door of the church, watching his mother move on to another relationship. And I was a vagrant priest and a failed writer.

But, of course, we too were entitled to some happiness. Some part in the fairytale of romantic love. I didn't want to spend all my life alone, shovelling last night's ashes into a bucket and staring into an empty fire grate with only myself in the room. I wanted company. I wanted someone to cling to. Someone to love.

And our marriage didn't go wrong. But time sucked the freshness out of it, as it sucks it from everything. We became used to each other. We folded around each other. We thought each other's thoughts and finished each other's sentences.

I wanted to leave her, even though I loved her. In my fifties I needed space to myself. Like all men of that age, I felt I was in the last-chance saloon. And I needed to push more. So I did. I pushed hard and bust my gut. I got sick and depressed. I spent six months lying in bed remembering the sorrows of childhood, and how my attempts to find meaning in life had all ended up in failure. I had been a Catholic priest for a short time and I had tried Buddhism

5

for seventeen years. I travelled as far as Mongolia in search of meaning, but in the end I was forced to let go of magical thinking altogether.

When I was sick, I became so helpless that for the first time in my life I began to rely on someone else. And, ironically, the someone else who happened to turn up was the woman I had left.

I was fifty-two, and I was desperate to leave her. To get away. And it was all because of the dishwasher. She would fill it to the brim. She would squash the dishes in so tight, they got damaged. They chipped around the edges. She would layer a further row of plates and pots on top of the ones that were in the allotted grooves. And then she would stuff cutlery in, and close the door and turn the knob. She said it wasn't the dishwasher that chipped the plates. They got chipped because I didn't put them in correctly.

So I started turning on the machine when it was half-full. That way nothing would get chipped. She'd come home before I had emptied it, and she'd open the door and say, 'You shouldn't put the dishwasher on until it's full.'

So I decided to leave. A man must have his own dishwasher. A man must be free. *I should have gone to Paris when I was young.* That's what I told myself, as I looked out on the beardy rushes of Leitrim. I could have rented a space of my own and filled my own dishwasher whatever way I wanted.

'What are you thinking?' she asked.

'Nothing,' I said, staring out the window. *Nothing I could actually tell you.* 'I'm just looking at the donkeys.'

At that time our daughter was eleven and used to play in those rushy fields with the four donkeys that lived in a hut behind the German's house, down at the foot of the hill. Each morning the German woman opened the stable door and the donkeys came out for the day. The male would climb up to the top of the hill, and look around as if he was scouting for dangerous predators that might disturb the tranquillity of the morning. When he was certain that the coast was clear, and there were no tigers or wolves to be seen, he'd raise his head and bare his teeth and let loose a screech that would tear the eardrums off a cat, which signalled to the other three that it was safe to come up the hill. Mammy donkey and the two baby donkeys then joined Daddy at the top, finding grass between the rushes or sheltering beneath a clump of gorse bushes when it rained.

Our daughter often sat among them, having donkey conversations. She told me once that the Daddy donkey had a special position under the bush, much like my place in the armchair beside the fire in our house. Patriarchy, she was observing, was as rampant among donkeys as it was among humans.

Not that patriarchy was the order of the day in our compound. Being a sculptor, my wife had a large studio at the end of the garden where she spent endless hours during the time of the dishwasher wars. Being a writer, I worked in a very small studio at the other end of the garden. So our life was based on an equal partnership. We loved each other dearly and our daughter twice as much, but familiarity breeds contempt, and we got slightly bored with one another. We got fed up looking at each other, across the table of chipped crockery, day in, day out, like two ageing donkeys.

9

But everything changed one winter's night in 2006.

My wife had gone away for the week, leaving me at home to mind the child, or the child to mind me. Whatever. The child, in her final year in primary school, lay by the fire all evening, drawing horses and playing with Sam the black Labrador, who was endowed, it has to be said, with enormous testicles. It was the testicles that had put me off short-haired dogs in the first place, though I gave in when the child was six. I had endured Sam's devotion to personal hygiene for five years without complaining. But I drew the line when he farted in the house. Which he did on this particular evening, as the child lay her head on his flank. She burst out laughing, and I left the room, saying I was going to my bedroom to read my biography of the Dalai Lama in peace and quiet.

A few minutes later, she knocked on the door and asked if she could talk. I put down the book and she lay beside me and we both stared at the ceiling. This was a common event. We called it our Conversation Club. She often talked in a dreamy way about all her hopes for the future as we gazed at the ceiling.

'I'd love to be in a real show-jumping competition someday,' she said, only half-joking. Not unusual because she'd had a passion for horses from the age of four, probably brought on by long afternoons spent under the gorse bush talking to the donkeys. And she rode an old pony called Caesar, who was probably older than me, in the local equestrian centre.

'But I'd love to jump in real competitions,' she said again.

'Of course you would,' I said, engrossed in how the Dalai Lama had got out of Tibet.

'No,' she said, 'I'd really love to jump in those big show-jumping competitions they have on the television.'

I said, 'To compete at a high level in show jumping,

you'd need coaching and top-class horses and lots of other things that are not available in Leitrim.'

'Where would I get them?' she asked.

'Well,' I said, 'there are some secondary schools that do equestrian sports, but sadly none of them are in Leitrim.'

I thought that was the end of the matter.

'I'll go and look for a school,' she said, heading for the computer in the front room. A few minutes later she screamed, and I ran out wondering had the dog done something terrible on the carpet, or what, but she was at the screen, gazing with awe at a website for Loreto College, Mullingar, and in particular a news item about the school show-jumping team that had won first prize in the Schools Tournament at Hickstead on two separate occasions in previous years

'Mullingar, Dad,' she exclaimed. 'Mullingar.'

Mullingar is a midland town almost an hour and a half from where we lived, but I realised I had opened up a conversation that was now out of control. The following morning after the bus had picked her up outside the gate, I phoned Loreto College, Mullingar and spoke with the school secretary, who told me that they didn't take boarders anymore, but that if we were moving to Mullingar and wishing to secure a place for our child in September, then we should have her enrolled immediately.

'The closing day for applications is Thursday,' she said. 'And there's an open day that evening. So if you want to come and have a look at the school, you could do it all together.'

The wife was in the Tyrone Guthrie Centre in Annaghmakerrig, County Monaghan, that week; a retreat for artists, where she had gone to chill out for a few days and get some new ideas for her work. So obviously I wasn't going to disturb her there. I drove the child to Mullingar after school on Thursday and we had huge pizzas with lots of olives in a fancy Italian restaurant on Dominic Street, where the waiters had black waistcoats and Italian accents. There was nothing subtle about my tactics: I was hoping that Mullingar life would impress her even before we arrived at the school.

But I need not have worried. The school seduced her. A bright world of carpets, flowers, big smiling girls in blue uniforms, and young perfumed teachers fussing to show her the science lab and the five sinks in the kitchen and the cookers where she could bake apple tarts in home economics classes and, most important of all, the PE teacher, in the alcove of the main hall, who was showing videos of the team's victories at Hickstead.

'Are you interested in horses?' the lady enquired.

'Oh yes,' the child said, beaming at her, and I knew there was no turning back.

All I had to do was explain this sudden leap in the child's career to my wife, who was still over in the Tyrone Guthrie Centre, filling her sketchbook with drawings. She returned on the Saturday evening after a good week of creative work. I opened a bottle of Bordeaux and served up as good a pasta as I could manage, and made sure we were both relaxed at the fire before I brought up the subject.

'Well,' she said, 'any news?'

To my relief she was delighted with the idea of Mullingar and took it with enthusiasm. She too had been wondering what would happen at the end of our daughter's time in primary school, and where we might find a good secondary that would suit her. She had also been wondering how long we could go on like Mutt and Jeff, at either ends of the garden policing each other's imaginations. It was one of those moments in my life when I rejoiced in the fact that I had married an artist; a woman open to all sorts of crazy ideas and possibilities. And Mullingar was only an hour and twenty minutes away. I could rent a place there and use it for work, and the child could stay with me and we'd both be home at the weekends. Sure it wasn't as if I was going to Paris.

'It's brilliant news,' she declared. And, of course, we never mentioned the dishwasher.

13

I kissed her goodbye, and drove off in a red Ford Ka to Mullingar, where I had an appointment with an auctioneer in the afternoon. It was 16 June 2006, less than two months before my fifty-third birthday. There was nothing selfish in my plan. After all, it was a joint decision. And we were doing it for the child. She needed a good school where she could pursue her equestrian hobby. And we were doing it because we were artists and needed separate spaces to be creative. Of course. In fact, we were getting away from each other to improve the relationship. No way was this separation going to be the beginning of the end. Although as I drove out through Carrick-on-Shannon and onwards to Longford, the prospect of having my own space and my own independent life again after twelve years of marriage delighted me. I even turned off Joe Duffy's talk show and sang old songs to myself that I hadn't sung in years.

The auctioneer was a boy in a suit. A grey suit, a pink shirt and a blue tie. Obviously a mandarin invented in the good years of the Tiger. Though neither him nor I knew just then that the Tiger days were about to come to an abrupt end.

The dining room overlooked a gated courtyard. There were blocks of apartments on four sides. Polish children played below. I signed a one-year lease. And the daughter joined me in the first week of September.

It was the beginning of a new life for me. Mullingar, I told myself, could be the Prague of Ireland, a place close to almost anywhere else in the country. A town of sophistication beyond the wildest dreams of Leitrim's ageing bachelors.

And it was a genuine Celtic Tiger apartment. There was a kitchenette off the main living area with an air extractor above the cooker – but that was just for show; it didn't actually extract air. So when frying the breakfast that winter, I kept the window open to prevent the smoke alarm going off. And that let in rain onto the worktop. And the rail for the curtains on the main window of the dining area was screwed into plasterboard and it collapsed after a few days and was never fixed. I never saw the auctioneer again. My money went into his account and that was the end of our relationship. He said he'd get the washing machine fixed, and I phoned him almost every week, but it was November before someone came to examine it.

And none of the doors had been hung right. They were all warped. And they didn't close properly. In particular, the bathroom door was dangerous, because it had no safety lock. And if the key was turned, there was a great possibility that it might never open again. This didn't matter to my daughter, as girls of her age don't lock bathroom doors anyway, and I was ever vigilant. Until the week before Hallowe'en. I was alone in the building, and fancied a shower in the afternoon. I undressed in the bedroom, waddled around with a towel for a few minutes looking for conditioner, hopped into the steaming shower and scrubbed away for ten minutes before it dawned on me that I had automatically turned the key.

In panic, I tested the lock. It wouldn't open. I was naked, and my phone was outside on the bed. I imagined my daughter coming from school at 4 p.m. and trying to get access from outside, and wondering where Daddy might be. And eventually the police coming perhaps, and finding Daddy in the loo with no clothes on. I was getting very stressed.

Fortunately there was a floor mop in the corner beside the shower. I used the long plastic handle like a lance and took one run at the door, piercing a hole in the MDF. Once I could actually see out, it was only a matter of time, picking bit by bit with my fingers, and then my full claw, until I had a hole in the door big enough to climb through.

Other than that, the apartment was lovely.

I delighted in listening to the traffic in the morning as I lay in bed, reminding myself that I was no longer stuck in the wilds of the countryside but in an exciting and vibrant urban environment.

And my daughter was absolutely no bother. We lived in parallel universes, crossing each other's paths on only the most necessary of occasions. Usually to do with survival. She'd get hungry and I would feed her.

I drove her to school in the rush hour each morning and had the apartment to myself for the day. I strolled about town and drank real coffee made by a girl from Warsaw at a street café. There were two of them behind the counter, with blonde hair and high boots, dispensing lattes and espressos.

'How are you today, Michael?' Olga would ask, when she got to know me.

'I'm good today, Olga. And I believe it's going to be a nice day.'

'Yes,' she said, 'better than yesterday. Yesterday was rain.'

'Yes, rain,' I agreed. 'But not today. Today just clouds.'

'Yes,' Olga said, laughing. 'Clouds. Today.'

I will admit that it wasn't a hugely nuanced conversation, but it was music to my ears. The foreign accents and the

17

affability of half a dozen girls behind various counters, in Gala shops, coffee shops, and the newsagent's across the street, contributed to what I believed was the new cosmopolitan adventure on which I was embarking.

Usually the coffee shops were full of country people from places like Castlepollard and Killucan, and the weather was cold and grey, but I didn't care. An old lady who always carried Dunnes Stores shopping bags was a regular in the café, for the pot of tea, and she tried to discuss Joe Dolan with me a few times. Nothing very sophisticated about that, but then I didn't know much about Joe. So I avoided her.

And at least I could say that the apartments around me were very cosmopolitan, most of them rented by Polish or Lithuanian couples. Their children played in the courtyard. And though they weren't allowed have pets, one of the Polish children had a fluffy little mutt that she walked in the evenings around the courtyard, and brought to the underground car park to do his toilet. In fact, the Irish couple in the apartment above me also had a dog and they weren't so fussy about where he did his toilet. They drove a flashy car, and I once saw their little mutt on the grille of a balcony relieving himself. They dressed like rock stars, and wore sunglasses, and as far as I was concerned, they were just another example of the cultural vitality of Mullingar and the life that had opened up for me.

My child went to school in her blue uniform, and came home and ate soup and went out to ride a horse in an equestrian centre. She came home again and ate dinner and did her homework and went to bed. And I could manage all that without disrupting my fantasy world. The wife arrived on Friday evenings, and we lived a full and normal life again and she did most of the running around with the daughter to show-jumping competitions. We had an old wooden horse box, which was hitched to the back of the wife's van, and Annabelle, a sweet grey pony with long black eyelashes, steadied herself within, as the wife negotiated the byroads of the midlands in search of various fields, fetes and ShowJumping Ireland (SJI) competitions.

But on Sunday afternoons my wife packed her computer into the car, waved to me as the gates under the arch opened automatically, and drove away. I was separated again. A man on the streets of Europe. Almost.

By the summer of 2007, I was pushing myself. I was getting old. I sensed time running out. I was in the last-chance saloon. Not focused about where I should push, but I pushed anyway. For example, I replaced the small Ford Ka with a Grand Pajero Jeep, a black long-axle machine that I believed suited the times we lived in. I couldn't really afford it, but that didn't seem to be an important consideration at the time. The country was awash with money. A jeep especially suited me in the fast lane of the urban social jungle. And I was also hungering for more than just a latte and a brief chat about the weather. I was pushing my way socially, trying to find some vague destiny among the well-heeled, four-wheeler, horsy ladies of Westmeath, where the stallions are all prizewinners.

In July, I was invited to a posh dinner party in a mansion on the outskirts of town, surrounded by flat fields, tall beech trees and the occasional chestnut, bouncing into watery green bloom. The evening sun lit up the green lawns and the low red-bricked walls around the tiled patio. The company included a businessman and a beautiful actress, who stopped everyone in their tracks with her rendition of 'Ride On', and the lead singer from a rock band. One guest had a house in Italy. Even before the cocktails were finished, I was overexcited. As we moved inside for the main course – a fish cooked to a Spanish recipe – I was dangerously flushed with Gordon's gin.

There was a blonde-haired woman at the table and I could not take my eyes off her. She moved about as if she was sleepwalking. And long after the desserts and coffee, as music played in the lounge and animated guests sat around a table just inside the patio discussing nurses' pay, I made my approach. She was in the kitchen slicing lemons. I placed a wok on my head and petitioned her to smile for an errant knight. She may not have read Cervantes, but even Don Quixote wearing a shaving basin instead of a helmet could not have appeared so pathetic. I slurred my admiration for her beauty as she twisted the lemon into her glass at the kitchen worktop and the drops fell one by one.

I made a melancholy lament for my lost youth, saying that I had spent too long in remote Leitrim as a married man but was now embarking on the adventure of a lifetime, and that she was the most beautiful woman I had ever seen or could hope to encounter in all of Europe. I gushed on about her feminine charms, and in particular her earlobes, upon which I had focused, much to her annoyance.

'Take that wok off your head,' she said. 'It's not funny.' She walked away towards the lounge with ice clinking in her crystal glass.

I was sick for three days afterwards and too embarrassed to go out of doors. By Wednesday, I felt strong enough to venture out for a spin in the jeep, wearing sunglasses. Over the months in Mullingar, I had discovered that in such moments of shame, a spin in the jeep could provide great consolation.

It enabled me to connect with my nomadic self. I could hug the steering wheel and escape all relational distress or financial pressure or social shame and head down the N4 like a Mongol on horseback, watching the earth stretch before me. Behind the steering wheel, I embraced a myth and was swelled by an unseen hero. I became a homeless hunter, drifting alone where neither God nor social decorum could restrain me. I was only going to Athlone, which is not quite Route 66, but I had visions of a fresh bun and a good coffee before driving home through Kilbeggan. That night I analysed it all with the barman, an overweight Buddha who

21

pulled my pints; a dour guru with moustache and drooping eyes who had become my only companion in this new world.

He leaned across the counter and said, 'Your problem started when you threw out the rabbit ears. You've too many channels. You don't get out often enough.'

There was a time when I thought the guttural sound of the Russian tongue was like ice breaking and about as erotic as the frosty dead eyebrows of Leonid Brezhnev. But two tall women farther down the bar were changing my mind. My ears were wagging and my libido was going into spasms and I could hardly hear what the barman was saying.

'Either go back to your wife in Leitrim,' he said, 'or else get out more often. You're just sitting there brooding. There's more to life than *EastEnders*.'

'I watch other stuff besides soap operas,' I said.

'Look,' he said, 'yo-yoing up and down to the video shop doesn't constitute a healthy option. You need to get out and meet people.'

'You mean fuck people,' I said in a whisper.

Then he leaned over the bar into my ear, and said confidentially, 'Take a crack at one of them.' He pointed at the Russians.

The thought terrified me.

I said, 'I do go out. In fact, I'm just back from a spin in the jeep.'

'Where did you go?' he asked.

'Athlone,' I said.

'That's sad,' he said.

I always hoped I'd fall in love. And if I grew up and fell in love, life would be easy. That's what I thought. But I grew up in Ireland, and it sometimes seems that Irish people have no hope. We live in despair. For women, the great disappointment is men; for men, it's practically everything. Everybody lives in despair. Which is odd for a nation so devoted to religion down the centuries. Or perhaps it's not.

Perhaps it's because of the weather or the Great Famine or because of the awful things that happen in Ireland over and over again. People grew too cynical to hope in anything. And without hope, I suppose, it's difficult to find love. Or maybe it's because the religion we cling to doesn't work anymore, and we are too afraid to say so. We are not a lazy people, but we are notorious for taking things easy.

That is until the days of the Celtic Tiger. We got our courage then. The nation couldn't be kept silent at dinner parties and gala nights, baring its collective soul about the need to push. Push the life. Push the job. Push the relationship. Push every button. Push the ATM machine. Push for promotion. Push yourself. Everybody. All together. Push. And I pushed. For years in Mullingar, I pushed.

Until I exploded.

Blew up, like an overheated, under-oiled engine. 'Stormy weather' is another way of saying it.

'I hear you ran into a bit of stormy weather,' someone said to me, after I had fallen apart. When I ended up in hospital and subsequently at home in bed, depressed for months. *Stormy weather*. I suppose that's it all right. Turbulence in the interior. Rain storms in the organics. And mental darkness. The consequences of pushing too much and ending up ill.

Afterwards I cried for a year. It was a good cry. It was a cry that allowed me to remember who I was. 'I am a bit like Sancho Panza,' I concluded. 'I cry a lot and I like donkeys.'

I loved riding the big-eared, furry beasts when I was a child, on the beach at Bundoran, with a gypsy boy holding the reins and my father holding my hand. And the cross on the donkey's back amazed me. I thought it was really put there by God's finger one morning when no one was looking to mark the donkey as a hero.

To me the donkey was something especially loved by God, and so it never bothered me when someone said, 'You made a bit of an ass of yourself last night.'

I did. Last night. And last year. And the year before that. Year after year, I ruined my life. I made the wrong decisions. I took the wrong road.

When I was in primary school, where the teachers used to beat us with canes and belts, my greatest consolation was to sit alone beneath the stairs in a dark cupboard and recite the lines of Chesterton's poem about the donkey which I had first learned in fourth class.

When fishes flew and forests walked
And figs grew upon thorn,
Some moment when the moon was blood
Then surely I was born;
With monstrous head and sickening cry
And ears like errant wings,
The devil's walking parody
On all four-footed things.
The tattered outlaw of the earth,
Of ancient crooked will;
Starve, scourge, deride me: I am dumb,
I keep my secret still.

Donkey. It's not an old word. In fact, it only came into use in the late eighteenth century. The older word was 'ass'. And when the *r* in 'arse' was silenced like a stone turned smooth in the flow of a river, the 'ass' was for reasons of propriety renamed a donkey. But I'll stick to 'ass'. I like to say, 'I'm an ass.' And, 'You're an ass.' I like to suppose that the future will be good for the donkey and me. We shall inherit the earth.

When my health broke down in 2011, people said, 'You're the right ass. What happened to you?' Just the same as they had said it when I was a child. I'd fall into the ditch and someone would say, 'Well, you're an awful ass.'

I believe my breakdown had been threatening for a long time. There was a flaw inside me from the beginning. In school Fr Fingers called me an ass. He was a teacher. He'd say, 'You can run but you can't hide, ye jack-ass.' I wasn't hiding. I had my head down. But he said that was hiding.

'Where's your homework?'

It wasn't done. I couldn't understand it. But I didn't say that.

I said, 'Please, Father, I forgot to do my homework.'

That's what we all said. No point in saying, *Please, Father, you're such a lousy teacher that no one in the class knows how to do the homework.*

'You forgot?'

And then he'd shove the glasses up his nose and say,

'Now, tell me this and tell me no more: are you an ass or am I an ass?'

And I'd say, 'I don't know, Father.'

Fr Fingers helped hundreds of children to hate school. He had a nickname for the bishop – Fr Eyebrows he called him. When he said it, we were all supposed to laugh. He licked his lips before slapping people and he relished his power over us.

I farted once too loudly, and he came down to me and said, 'And who have we here?' Because he prided himself on not knowing the pupils in his class.

I spoke my name.

'And are you an ass?'

'I don't know, Father.'

'Speak up,' he roared.

'I don't know, Father.'

'I told you yesterday,' he continued, 'when you forgot to do your homework, to go home and ask your mother were you an ass. Did you ask her?'

'No, Father.'

'Or maybe your mother thinks your teacher is an ass. And now you're farting like the ass that ate the turnips, so I'm asking you again – are - you - an - ass? Or am I an ass? And you still tell me you don't know.' He was roaring.

'I don't know,' I said again, stubbornly, because he wanted to shame me into saying, *Yes, Father, I must be an ass, because of the way I smell or because of my stupidity or*

27

because of my intellectual limitations. Father, I must be the biggest jackass in the room.

'One of us must be an ass,' he declared. 'And it's certainly not me.'

The class laughed, and it was over. He had delivered a punch line to his own satisfaction.

But other pupils endured worse. Sometimes when a boy failed repeatedly to achieve any success at his homework, Fr Fingers would oblige him to stand before the class and heehaw, and we would all feel tainted by the shame. So we all failed Fr Fingers. And as life went on, I failed more and more. I failed regularly and to greater degrees. And I failed at everything. Or at least a little voice inside me said that. A little Fr Fingers was sitting inside on his throne, mumbling away around the clock.

Mammy wasn't much help either. She was always threatening to leave, and so I felt I was constantly letting her down. I remember her in the hallway at home in Cavan, putting on her red coat one afternoon.

'I'm going to throw myself in the river,' she said. This was a common enough threat.

'I'd be better off at the bottom of a lake.'

It's not that she was suicidal or anything. It was just a tactical threat; a dramatic way of letting off steam and getting me into line. I realised this later. But I didn't know it when I was four. I became hysterical and screamed and begged her not to go. So she relented.

'If you're good, I'll stay,' she said, and I promised with all my heart to be good and she put her keys back on the hall table and her red coat back under the stairs.

One day in Clerys in Dublin, she actually did vanish. She went missing. She was heading for the lingerie department in the basement, and she forbade me to come with her. I was left standing at the door, staring at a woman with a pram on the street who was selling newspapers. After what seemed like a week, I turned around and went into the shop to find Mammy. But she was gone. Vanished. She wasn't anywhere in the lingerie section. I could see knickers and bras and corsets, but no Mammy. I started crying and a staff person in a suit came over and said, 'What's the matter?'

'I am looking for Mammy,' I said. 'But Mammy's gone.'

A few minutes later, I heard my name announced over the Tannoy and saw my mother emerge from the section where the bridal gowns were displayed. It was a long time ago. A time when small cylinders like tin cans shuttled back and forth on wires from the counters to the central cashier with money and change and receipts and women wore corsets and skirts below their knees. But even then it was clear to me that love was the most important thing in the world, and that eventually I must fall in love with someone who would never disappear.

Depression usually got in the way, even in the dance halls where I jived and the carnival tents where I spent summer

29

nights sweating and drinking lemonade with plump girls from remote country areas I had never heard of. I suppose I was always depressed. There was always something inside me which drew me away from the outside world and left me restless and uneasy. In the past year I've discussed the subject with therapists, but they say I must find peace within myself. Over the years, I've tried two religions and no religion, and nothing seems to bring lasting peace. Although until last year, the restlessness or unease in my heart didn't worry me. I thought it was normal. In fact, I didn't even know I was depressed. I thought I was just sad. A melancholic creature with too many secrets.

When I met the love of my life, my sadness dissolved. She had black hair and dark eyebrows. Her mouth was firm and strong. Her eyes explored me in detail, physically, and though she wasn't smiling, she wasn't judging me either. It was a gaze of intensity and curiosity. She was very curious, and something in me attracted her attention. 'That,' I told myself, 'is a plus.'

I liked her shoulders a lot. They had a firmness where her back curved into her neck. A stockiness in her genes that was reinforced by long days in stone yards and in her studio, chipping dust off limestone with a chisel. She wore goggles and white overalls, like an industrial cleaner handling chemicals or a state pathologist. There was nothing girly about her. She watched me warily as if I were a hunter. Her posture was defiant, and her eyes said *I'm a hunter too*.

It was a long time ago that I first gazed at her. She was on the grass outside the main door of the Tyrone Guthrie Centre. I could have avoided the moment. Shied away from the encounter. Kept my head down like I did when Fr Fingers hovered, but a voice inside me, akin to a wise man at the back of a cave, whispered, 'If you miss this moment, you will miss your life.' I would hardly call it love at first sight. Far from it. But I was staring at her. And she gazed back. It was August 1984.

'What are you looking at?' she asked. I couldn't formulate an answer immediately. I was poleaxed. In such trepidation that I couldn't speak. Held catatonic by the interior weather; my life flashing before me, or at least certain moments of it.

When I was seventeen a girlfriend said, 'Your eyes never smile. Even when your face pretends.' When I was twenty-three, I went to an island to visit a wise man who was a writer. As we walked on the heather by the ocean he said, 'Every man must walk over a cliff.'

I presumed he meant it in the sense of taking risks.

'Oh you're right there,' says I.

'Blindfolded,' he added. 'A man must walk over the cliff blindfolded!' He was animated. The wind around his head. 'And regularly,' he roared.

To walk over a cliff blindfolded didn't seem to me such a wonderful idea. To fall into the abyss and accept it willingly sounded daft. To drive oneself to the edge like a mad cow, to seek the cliff, to jump off with blinded eyes! Jesus, I thought, some of these writers are not right in the head.

But I was only twenty-three. I'd had a sheltered childhood and knew very little. In fact, I didn't even know that women had breasts until I was nine. I had not learned anything about the breast from my mother, except that cows' teats were apparently dirty. We were in Gowna one afternoon visiting remote relations who farmed by the side of the Arva road, and I was in the backyard tucked underneath an old cow, fingering her udder with fascination. 'Come out of there this minute,' my mother declared, 'that's dirty.'

My mother raged at her own fireside for years, disillusioned with life. In her wedding photographs, she smiles with abandon beneath a flowery white hat, though she wears a cream suit rather than a bridal gown. Her husband, a much older man, looks out from the same photographs with uncertainty, as if he was wondering, *Who got me into this?*

I always dreamed of being a writer. When I was a teenager, my most treasured possession was an old typewriter that my Uncle Oliver gave me for my fifteenth birthday. I wrote poems and sent them to 'New Irish Writing' in the *Irish Press*. Some of them were published. In my twenties, I kept the dream alive in cardboard boxes beneath the bed, full of embarrassing, self-indulgent short stories and melancholic poems about loneliness. But in 1980, I won a Hennessy Award for a story in the *Irish Press*, and I began to look seriously at the possibility of being a full-time writer.

By 1984, I had enough material for my first book, and so I applied to the Tyrone Guthrie Centre at Annaghmakerrig for a residency. To my delight, I was offered a four-week residency at the centre to finish what turned out to be my first book.

The Tyrone Guthrie Centre at Annaghmakerrig was a new and strange world to me. A temporary asylum for writers and painters in the heat of creative thought or in flight from broken relationships and seeking a few weeks' respite to get their heads sorted. A centre of coherent novelists and world-famous piano players sitting side by side with unwashed hippies trading off some slim volume of useless poetry published years earlier.

As I pushed the bike up the last hill to the front of the big house, a small cluster of artists and writers in sunglasses and straw hats were picnicking on the lawn, sipping lemon drinks and eating cheese and bread and smoked fish. I introduced myself as the new resident.

'Are you a poet?' someone enquired.

'No,' I replied, 'I'm a novelist.'

'Ohh, a novelist. How amazing. What have you written?'

'Nothing,' I confessed. 'I'm hoping to finish my first book.' After all, I was only thirty-one years old. As far as I was concerned, life was still ahead of me.

There was an uncertain silence for a while among the artists and I refused to offer further information because I didn't want to give away any secrets. A pianist was practising in the music room, scattering Beethoven sonatas across the lawn. There was a famous poet, whose face and voice I knew from television, two American novelists, a mid-western academic in his forties and a deeply melancholic woman from New York, who saw through me instantly and almost wept the moment we shook hands. Were it not for the fact that she was thirty years older than me, she might have been the person with whom I could have spent the rest of my life. And there was a dark-haired woman, on the fringes of the party, staring at me.

The picnic was spread out on a tartan rug and directly above it was a window, from where came a sudden whine.

'No,' someone was saying in a cut-glass Dublin accent, 'I'm not taking off my clothes again. I did it yesterday.'

'It's the painters,' the old American woman explained. 'They have life drawing classes every day.'

And the mid-western academic sneered, as he sat on a wicker chair, smoking, as if life drawing was a ridiculous idea.

It was a rambling old house where Sir Tyrone Guthrie once played cards with his half-blind mother, and where Alec Guinness once rehearsed *Hamlet* in the nursery. Dancers, stage designers, acrobats, American academics from unheard of universities. And women. Women painting flowers. Women painting vaginas. Women making sculpture. Women talking about women. Women talking about feminism. Feminists talking about women.

35

Everybody talking about misogyny. And unshaven old men with pee stains on their trousers talking about books they wrote decades earlier. Annaghmakerrig was a strange place.

And one particular woman with dark hair and a powerfully intense presence walked through it all with an air of indifference. As if she couldn't care what big shot owned it, or who lived there now or what they were talking about. There was a touch of carelessness in the way she drank her tea or tossed the leaves into the sink or left the washed cup upturned on the drying rack. She knew the world sensately. She was having no illusions about the interior of things. The world was clear to her. *Imagine those fingers on my body*, I thought, as I sat across from her on the lawn, staring straight at her.

The director of the centre Bernard Loughlin told me to take the front bedroom upstairs, over the drawing room. 'You're lucky,' he said. 'It's the best room, but someone cancelled this morning. And don't make any noise going up. There's an old writer having a siesta in the room across the corridor.'

I followed his instructions and opened the door of my room as quietly as I could and found a big black cat sitting curled up on the bed. I was delighted. Not so much by the cat as by the window, which looked onto the front of the house, and where I could still see the artists, the poets and the writers, and the dark-haired woman who had been looking at me. There was a writing desk in the corner, and a chaise longue and a standard lamp. Two windows looked out on a small lake, green drumlins and forestry. There was a modern double bed in the corner, but other than that the furniture in the room suggested the 1930s. My typewriter was already positioned on the writing desk, where I hoped all the important moments of the next few weeks would occur. In the middle of my old-fashioned room there was a steel winding staircase that I was fearful to ascend all afternoon, wondering what was up there. Eventually when I did get to the top, I found a shower room, all enclosed in wood, and painted green and red. I had never felt in awe as I showered, and returned down the staircase with a towel slung around my waist. I lay on the bed and listened to the sound of an electric saw in the distance, and I guessed that someone was cutting the evergreen spruces in the forest. My bags weren't even unpacked. Through the open window I could see the woman with the dark hair sitting on a rug with other artists. I could hear birds, bees and the sound of a spade in the flowerbeds hitting something hard. The gardener had hit a rock with his spade and was tapping it to determine what it was. Maybe it was a rock. Maybe not. One way or another he was determined to dig it out, and the incident was recounted that evening at the dinner table by one of the guests.

'Apparently,' one artist explained, 'the rock turned out

37

to be bits of coal in a fertiliser bag. A fertiliser bag if you don't mind!'

'A thing of exquisite beauty,' someone else said savagely. 'It ought to be in a museum.' And a third artist speaking quietly said, 'Can you imagine the amount of fertiliser the local farmers put on the land around here. And it's not needed. It gets washed into the lake and the lake sometimes glows in the dark because there are so many chemicals in it.'

Everyone around the table had muttered their agreement, and their astonishment that peasants could be so thick as to overdose the land with fertiliser and then just cast away the plastic bags into what was once the vegetable garden of the big house; clearly we were surrounded by Philistines.

I didn't know much about fertiliser. And, to be honest, I have probably been careless about where I've thrown plastic bags on more than one occasion over the years. So at the table, I learned to be careful. It was obvious to me that I was a Philistine, and I could give myself away quite easily if I wasn't careful.

But that was a small price to pay for being allowed enjoy the wonderful world of privilege, and artistic possibility that existed in the house. The evergreen spruces also came up at the dinner. Apparently when the chainsaw stirs into life, the deer come and stand around, because they associate it with the felling of trees and the flaking of the bark which they love to eat.

'How amazing,' someone said.

Annaghmakerrig was like that. People didn't talk ordinary talk. They swapped amazing nuggets of information and wonderful anecdotes about their travels in exotic countries or offered insights into life that no one had previously considered. I never thought I'd be accepted to the centre, but there I was showered, naked, lying on a double bed, listening to the sounds of summer float in the window – and already thinking about that beautiful, dark-haired woman with the sculptor's chisels. And it was good to be clean again because I had pedalled a bike in the August heat from Fermanagh, sixteen miles away, with a rucksack of clothes strapped to the crossbar and Uncle Oliver's typewriter on the carrier.

The gong in the hall went dong-dong-dong at 7 p.m., and that first evening I helped the old writer down the stairs. Twelve people sat around the long table in the kitchen, passing back and forth salad bowls and casseroles of meat and bowls of warm aubergines.

'There's a draught in my room,' the old writer grumbled. It was clear that he was the most important beast in the room and that he would be leading the conversation for the evening. He quoted from his books every so often, and mentioned international writers as if they were old friends or fools.

I was trying to name the foods, many of which I'd never seen before. Home-made tagliatelle and aubergines both frightened me. And I'd never seen flowers in a salad before. I kept my head down, said nothing and hoped no one

39

would notice me, or ask about what I did in the real world besides dream of writing books.

Dinner was compulsory each evening and I suffered enormous stress after a few days, trying to remain invisible, with my eyes cast down – Fr Fingers inside me knitting a shroud from my guts. The sophistication was absolutely terrifying. I was shaking with fear as people with cut-glass accents chatted about restaurants in Tokyo and Zurich. But what really alarmed me was the way they talked about Catholicism. A day didn't pass without some anecdote arising which illustrated the misogynistic anti-intellectual core of the Irish Church, and the artists around the table got puffed up every night with indignation about the immorality and duplicity of bishops in relation to abortion, divorce and contraceptives. It's fair to say that at the time in Ireland women were furious with the Church's abuse of power, and rightly so.

I wanted to put my hands up. I wanted to confess. Each day in my room, I would talk to the mirror and persuade myself that it was time to speak out. To tell them the truth. But by the time I got to the table, the conversation would be in full flow, and the righteous anger on everyone's lips left me cowering with shame. My lovely residency in the big house was turning into a nightmare. Instead of feeling happy to be finally writing a book, and living among other writers, I was mortified. And the longer I kept the secret, the harder it was to speak it. Nobody yet knew what I was

40

carrying. How could I begin to explain it?

I was a priest. If I had long ears and the donkey's head that Bottom was bestowed with by Puck in Shakespeare's play, I could not have been more miserable. It would have been less shameful.

But this is a love story. And to think of Annaghmakerrig, thirty years later, still fills me with tenderness. The big house in the lonely drumlins. The still lake. The wooded parkland. The bees buzzing around the flowers. The ghost of Guthrie in the shadows at night, never far from my shoulder. His breath behind me on the stairway in every draught. His big white mug on the shelf in the kitchen. His binoculars on top of the piano in the drawing room where Judith, his wife, hid her bottle of gin for years after he died. His walking sticks and old boots still inside the hall door. His family photographs in the drawers. His long-playing records strewn about beneath the sofa.

That great big man had died only thirteen years earlier, one morning while he was cutting rhododendron bushes along the avenue, which were still flourishing in 1984 when I first walked there with the dark-haired woman. I was in his house. In his rooms. In his things. I could find his name written on books. His face in dozens of family photographs on the sideboard. His spirit of adventure and the power of his creativity in the air I was breathing. That colossus drank wine with Alec Guinness at the very same bay window where I first met the dark-haired woman and he rehearsed

Hamlet with Alec in the room where the pianist was now practising Beethoven. It was all too much for me. Too overwhelming. Too wonderful.

I got started on my book. I applied myself for four hours every morning and walked in the grounds every afternoon. One very hot day, I went swimming in the lake with the American woman who was too old for me, though I found her beautiful, especially in the water, where her body became young again and her long grey hair turned black and shone like a young girl.

And on another occasion, I cycled to the Kesh Bar with a tall and elegant English woman who had just broken up with her husband. She wore a straw hat, even while cycling, and she had a backpack to carry bottles of vodka from Cootehill, which she drank alone in her room, or at the bay window in the drawing room, in her straw hat during cocktail hour, hoping someone or anyone would join her. One evening she invited me into her company after the meal and I drank with her till dawn and then she took me out on the lake in a small boat. We stopped at the far shore and I mentioned that Guthrie and his wife used to make fires there and sit around stark naked.

'How do you know? she asked.

'I read it in Alec Guinness's book,' I said.

'I hope you're not suggesting anything,' she said.

Of course I wasn't. For me it was good to have one ally at the table and, for her, I was a solace, as she grieved for her lost love and poured alcohol on the flames of her anger, as if that was going to put out the fire. And besides, she left a few days after I arrived.

I had seen nothing of the dark-haired woman for about a week. She was never at the table and nobody spoke about her, and then suddenly she reappeared. We were enjoying a bean curry one evening when she came in late, in a black overall, and almost unnoticed. But I saw a brooding shadow in her eyes like a wonderful lake under clouds, and lanterns of brown under her skin. She was like the wood of a walnut tree. The darkness of a forest. The stillness of a panther. And from the moment she spoke, I was hers.

The fact was that she didn't fit in. She was not one of them. She was trying to negotiate the salad bowl and nobody had introduced her. Nobody noticed her.

'What do I have to do around here to get some attention?' she said suddenly.

Everyone went silent. She wasn't even posh. And she had my undivided attention. I got more attracted to her as the evening wore on, and later, as the entire troupe walked to the pub, I lingered on the edge of the group, making up conversations with her in my head. But I had not yet spoken to her. And I didn't speak in the pub either. I was too busy drinking.

At about midnight, everyone walked back to the big house with bottles of Black Bush and collected in the drawing room, some sitting in a circle around the bay window, some at the card table and others on the sofa. She was alone near another window, flicking through photographs. I approached her. I was by now utterly unable to formulate sentences.

'So,' she said, 'what have you to say?'

And I said, 'I think I love you.'

Maybe it was just that I had some hope of success with her. Whereas with the others I was terrified to open my mouth. Shame left me silent. Shame left me desperate. The woman in the straw hat was still in love with grief, and the woman who swam like a dolphin was too old when she was out of water. But this woman was still young and beautiful, with strong features and powerfully dark eyes that said *I'm nobody's fool.*

I didn't feel shame with her. And maybe that is where love begins. When someone can take away the shame and let you be who you are.

'Yes, I think I love you,' I said, like an idiot.

She looked at me warily, sipped her drink and said, 'That's bollocks.'

I had never said those words to another person in my life. I never said them to my mother. I'd never told my father I loved him, even when he was dying. Slept on and off with an American student for months at university who would whisper in my ear on the pillow over and over again, 'I love you' – and then would weep because I could never bring myself to the generosity of responding.

Of course there was drink on the table. Lots of drink.

44

In fact, I was plastered. But there was also an instantly recognisable tenderness between us. A feeling of ease, even in this comic satire of romance. And it sustained us. There was no one else in the room who mattered to me. Songs were sung. Arguments evolved. A writer fell on the floor and someone had to carry him to his room. But nothing could break the spell between us. After another few glasses of whiskey, I accompanied her upstairs and down the back corridor to her room.

Nothing had been said, or proposed or accepted. She just said, 'I think I'll head for my bed.' And I said, 'Yes, that's a good idea; so will I.'

We left the room together, went up the stairs and I followed her along her corridor and she didn't make any protest. She was in a back room beside the music room and when I stepped inside she locked the door and I thought, *Holy Jesus, this is it.*

Yet we did not make love. Instead, we stayed awake all night, with a shaft of light falling on the floor from the August moon. We stayed awake wondering who we were, and where we were coming from and what we were doing, and what was happening to us. Because something was happening to us. We were being born as twins. We were opening a tiny space in the universe where a couple can escape the loneliness that each individual is condemned to. Just for a few hours, we were in a space called 'us'. And it was wonderful and the dawn light on her body magnified

45

my lust. But still we did not make love. We just lay there. Awake and fearful, as the birds began their chorus on the far side of the lake, and even later, as the early-morning pianist began Beethoven's sonata in B minor.

'So what do you do besides writing?' she wondered, as we lay on the sheets and exchanged nuggets of biography. I had to put it out there. Put it on the table. Don't mess about. No matter how dreadful the consequences.

'I'm a priest,' I said.

I don't know what she thought of me at that moment because she didn't show it. She just looked straight at me, without the slightest expression. And we held each other there in that gaze for a long time, without quite knowing where this was going.

The priesthood embodied my depression. It was the glove. The wrap-around numb bodysuit that I put on to isolate myself from ordinary life.

I had gone to the seminary originally when I was eighteen, but stayed only one year. Then I did a BA as a lay student and became a teacher. After two years of that, I got a job in Sligo with Social Services, which lasted another year. And then at twenty-four years of age I returned to the seminary in Maynooth. I studied theology for four years and was ordained a priest in 1981 at the age of twenty-eight.

When most other young men were finding confidence in adulthood and deepening their experience of social relationships, particularly with women, I was on course for a life of splendid isolation.

Because being a priest certainly isolated me. Ordination was not an act of hope but one of despair. Celibacy was a declaration that I would remain without a lover for life, without all the consequent tenderness and intimacy that family ties nurture in a human being. I was like a suicide bomber, because celibacy was a sign of Paradise that I carried in my body. I said no to the flesh in slow motion over a lifetime, whereas suicide bombers do it with a bang.

And my act of renunciation was made in the name of heaven, signifying a defiant confidence in a future realm, in contrast to which all pleasures and comforts on earth paled into insignificance. I abandoned my identity and assumed the role of black-robed celibate male, a thing that has been a sign of contradiction in unconscious societies for centuries. And probably will continue to be for a long time, until eventually society wakes up, becomes more conscious and faces up to humanity's brief existential moment on earth. So, yes, perhaps even as a priest I was depressed but I didn't realise it.

The first morning I woke in my new parochial house, a modern bungalow, after being appointed to the parish of Derrylin in County Fermanagh, I looked out the window and saw an old woman standing in the porch of a grocery

48

and hardware store across the street. The following morning she was there again. A thin lady in a grey coat and scarf, with winged spectacles, like a character from the 1950s. It was only 6 a.m. But she stood for three hours, waiting until the shop opened at 9 a.m. And she was there again the following day. And every morning for a week. Then it stopped. And then, after a few more days, it began again. Maybe she has no clock, I thought, and the early dawn confuses her.

One day I was in the shop buying food for a rosebush and I asked the lady behind the counter about the early-morning customer.

'She's a bit odd,' the shopkeeper said.

'What does she buy?'

'Cat food. She has lots of cats. Too many if you ask me.'

One morning the old lady stared at me. I was behind the lace curtain of my bedroom, and she saw me. She must have noticed the curtain move, and she stared straight at me. Then she disappeared for most of the winter. It was in the spring of the following year that her neighbours came to me one day to say they were worried. The cats were crawling around inside the windows, and there had been no sign of her for days.

A flotilla of small boats was launched to search for her on Lough Erne, and I happened to be in the boat that finally found her beneath the bridge at Trasna Island, her chest bloated and her body badly damaged by briars, branches

49

of trees and fish. She was buried a few days later, with a scattering of neighbours in attendance. I threw the clay on her coffin and I took it personally. It was as if she had seen through me on those mornings when she stood across the road and looked straight at my lace curtains. As if she would have understood me. As if she might have told me the truth about myself, which is why perhaps I was afraid to visit her through the winter. I was afraid of her. Afraid of her feminine mystique and wisdom. Afraid of her madness. Afraid her presence might have had some message for my life. I had not paid her enough attention and I felt very badly about that.

So I paid more attention to other deaths. And there were plenty. Late one evening I helped drag a father out of a drain half a mile from his home. His last cigarette butt was floating on the surface of the water beside him. I saw a farmer lying in a field of hay one summer's day and helped his sons carry the body up to the house on the back of a door, the smell of rashers still lingering on the dead mouth. I saw a young man impaled on a buck rake that had moved when he was closing a gate behind his tractor. He was on a slope and he forgot to pull up the handbrake. The engine of the tractor was still warm when I arrived. I waited until dawn with a schoolteacher dying of cancer. I left the hospital at 5 a.m. and in the car park I could hear a thousand birds sing their chorus of joy to the new day. But I could not join them.

I touched dead faces, shovelled clay into open graves and tried as best I could to say comforting words to broken-hearted families.

I closed coffin lids and spaces inside my own heart that I never wanted to open again. And when I opened the front door of a dead house and saw the family members all dressed in black, with red eyes, sitting helplessly in a blue fog of tobacco smoke, I would summon up old clichés about God's will and heavenly peace, though the words were so archaic they stuck in my throat.

'Ah,' they would say, 'here's the priest. Thank God.'

But I only felt shame in their presence. I felt like a charlatan to be with them in their grief. Because it wasn't their grief that troubled me. And other than those duties that brought me close to the dead, there was little else to do in the swanky bungalow on a street in the middle of town. My ministry was about sick beds, tragic accidents and cemeteries. There was nothing else. I had a glasshouse of tomato plants and a garden of roses, which I had inherited from the previous curate. I had a cat, which gave birth to four kittens in a box beside the kitchen range. I lived without being hugged. The only parishioners who came close usually wanted to rebuke me for something radical I had said in a sermon, or for conducting confessions without wearing my proper clerical clothes. I was completely alone and had little interest in either tomatoes or roses, so even they began to wither. The roses got blackspot and the

51

tomatoes were drenched with greenfly by the time I packed my rucksack and took off on my bike for Annaghmakerrig.

Everything died in the end. One afternoon in November, I was rushing back to the local secondary school where I taught religion to teenage girls, and in my stress and anxiety not to be late, I reversed over three of the kittens.

That winter I phoned a local nurse half a dozen times from the floor of my bedroom where I was immobilised with pain in the back. She came and rubbed wintergreen into my muscles and helped me into bed. Her soft hands on my back were such a tenderness that on one occasion they brought me to tears. She pretended not to notice, and she joked about how I must have lifted too many coal buckets or sat too long at the desk leaning over the typewriter. And it was true. I did spend a lot of time that winter leaning over the typewriter, putting together a draft of the novel which I hoped was going to get me into the Tyrone Guthrie Centre, and eventually get me out of the priesthood forever.

The dark-haired woman remained in Annaghmakerrig for just one week. On the second night, I knocked on her door again and she let me in. She told me that one of the other artists had approached her during the day.

'What are you doing with that fucker?' the other artist had wanted to know. 'Don't you know he's a priest?'

But she wasn't going to be told what to do. In the days that followed, we took frequent walks by the lake and along the avenue of rhododendrons. I talked and she listened. And that was all that happened. We had slept together twice. Once in a state of wild abandon and high romance, and once like children, hungry for the consolation of physical intimacy. What pains she was seeking shelter from I didn't know and didn't ask. I knew she had a son, a family life, going on elsewhere. But I was only interested in her.

We didn't exchange addresses or phone numbers when she was leaving. I don't think we even said goodbye. One evening I arrived at table and realised she had left, and I had another two weeks on my own in the big house, my head bowed in shame most of the time as the righteous artists discussed the hideous deeds of Roman clerics. Fr Fingers was inside knitting my guts and reminding me that no matter what delusion I had of love for a few brief days, I was, and would remain, just as he had assured me when I was young, forever an ass.

Nor did I expect to hear from her again. She had her life and I had my parish in Fermanagh. So in September I returned to the bungalow, watched soap operas, delivered melancholic sermons to the postman and a few old ladies who came to ten o'clock mass on weekdays. I travelled around the hills and the lakeshore once a month, offering old and infirm creatures the bread of heaven, or driving them in and out to hospital appointments in Enniskillen.

That's how I met Brigid. The district nurse had left a message on my answering machine with Brigid's name and directions to her cottage up the mountains. The nurse had attended her for a sore leg. Brigid's husband had been removed to hospital and Brigid had asked the nurse to find her a priest.

Brigid was a small stout woman in her eighties, with thick glasses, hair on her chin and a mole on her cheek, and she was always laughing. I would have been happy to call her Grandmother. I spent hours in her shadowy cottage, a long building with a galvanised roof, as the kettle sang on the range and smoke billowed in our faces when she opened the door of the range to put on more turf. She asked me did I believe in ghosts. I said no. She confided in me that one time when she was married, her long-dead father had appeared to her in the bedroom, advising her that a cow was calving. She woke up, got out of bed, went down to the barn and arrived just in time to pull the new calf into life. Her husband asked her why she had got up and she just said, 'Daddy told me.'

'Wasn't that wonderful?'

'Yes,' I agreed. 'It was.'

She chuckled and bit a lump of currant bread.

'Do you dream, Father?' she enquired.

'No.'

Pause.

'I fell in love with a man on a bike,' she said, 'because nobody else had a bike at the time. And he played in a band and I would go out with him to the dances, and

I always remember the accordion and trumpet strapped to the rear seat of the bike and I'd be perched on the crossbar.'

In fact, her husband was strapped to a wheelchair in the hospital, but I imagined him sixty years earlier, a big-boned man, enfolding her small body on the bike's crossbar as he pedalled off to dances deep in the night. From the day the musician walked her to the altar, and she went with him up the hills on the back of a cart, her life had been full of music.

'I remember the way he used to straighten his dicky bow before going into the hall,' she said. 'That's when I decided to marry him. When I seen him straighten the bow, and remove the bicycle clips and fix his trousers, I said to myself, there's a neat man. The trousers were pressed like razor blades. And wasn't I right?'

The idea of sudden love arising out of the ground and altering the universe on the head of a man's ability to knot his bow tie encouraged me greatly. I drove her into the hospital once a week to see the musician, but he was fading fast. I drove her up the winding mountain path through snow drifts in December to the cottage she lived in and I thought the snow would sweep me, her and my Datsun Cherry into the ditch. I waited as she took a large key from her pocket and turned it in the rusting lock and when we went inside she struck a match to light the lamp, pumping the tiny handle as she held the flame to the paraffin wick

55

and the room glowed with soft yellow light. I imagined her as a young woman, and was almost overcome.

One frosty morning she was sitting outside the door on a chair with a pan of breadcrumbs that she tossed to the ravenous blackbirds and finches in the nearby bush. 'They talk to me,' she said. 'I think they're angels. But what do you think, Father? You should know.' She chuckled because she was only teasing me and she knew that I knew damn all about angels or anything else to do with the life hereafter, and even less about this life.

We talked about her husband a lot because we both knew he had only days to live. On the last night, she kissed him in the wheelchair. As she was leaving, the nurse said he wouldn't last till morning, but Brigid was too frail to stay or else she didn't see the need to be with him at the end. I drove her home. I watched her open the door with the big rusty key.

'I'll show you the bike,' she said, and she began searching in drawers. 'I only used that bike once. It was in winter, and the road along the lakeshore was waterlogged, but I cycled through it into Enniskillen to get a tooth pulled.'

She couldn't find the picture she was looking for, of her husband and the bike, but she brought out a framed photograph of him when he was young, standing erect with members of the band, holding their instruments at their sides. Her elbow moved across the surface of the glass, taking a little grime from it, so that I could see more clearly the gallant musician in his bicycle clips and bow tie. She wept a little as I looked at it, and then she put it back in the drawer with her birth certificate and her pension book and her tablets. The comrade of her life was dying in Enniskillen and yet, as she closed the door on me, I felt she was not in the slightest bit lonely in her cottage of paraffin lamps and old photographs. She was glad to see me leave, perhaps so that she could have her supper and go to bed. As I drove back to my parochial house, I kept thinking of her angels and birds and dreams, and if there was envy in me I would have envied her, because she was a woman in love. And I was a man who needed to change his life.

When we had planted her husband in the corner of the graveyard and she went away to stay with relatives in Sligo, I returned to the drudgery of parish life, having by then entirely forgotten about the dark-haired woman from the previous summer.

A few weeks after Christmas, I heard her voice on the 57 answering machine. I had just returned from a routine visit to the primary school, and the bungalow was bleak and full of grey January light. I had forgotten to order oil and the central heating was off. The fire grate was full of ashes from the previous night. I had the bucket in my hand when her voice spoke from the machine.

'It's me,' she said. 'Just calling to wish you Happy New Year.'

Click. And the voice was gone. No number. No detail.

And no mobile phones back then. But I played her message three or four times in the empty hall. The Panasonic answering machine sitting on a small white table just inside the hall door. I sat down beside the phone book and the bucket, and listened again and again. I shovelled ashes into the bucket and then settled two firelighters in the grate and touched them with a flaming match, and tossed a full bucket of coal onto the flame. The entire thing was absurd. She was an artist. A liberated woman. I was a priest. We were like oil and water.

In the bathroom, I looked in the mirror. 'With monstrous head and sickening cry and ears like errant wings, the devil's walking parody on all four-footed things.' That was me. An ass if ever there was one. I had made a fundamental mistake when I became a priest, and now it was too late to drag myself out of it. Fr Fingers stirred inside me and agreed. 'You're dead right,' he said. 'For once.' And then something happened that I didn't expect.

One morning in February, I was having porridge in the kitchen when I heard gunshots outside. I went to the front door and saw a van drive away from the school bus on the other side of the street. Masked men with guns were in the back of the van, and they shot and cheered and yahoo-ed as they drove away from the bus. The bus driver was lying dead on the floor of the bus in a pool of his own blood.

By mid-afternoon journalists had arrived. When they asked me questions, I told them what I had seen. I described the men roaring in the back of the van. The cheers from the gunmen. That night on the news, it was the main headline. *Gunmen roaring yahoo as they leave the scene.* The story was personal. It revealed something about the killers. They weren't disciplined. They were full of sweaty vengeful lust, and, as they went away, were as delighted as football fans when a goal had been scored.

When Colm Tóibín was writing a book sometime later entitled *Bad Blood: A Walk Along the Irish Border*, he came to visit me and asked me to tell the story again. I repeated it once more.

'What did they shout?' he asked.

'Yahoo!'

'Say it the way they said it.'

So I shouted it. 'Yahoo.'

He seemed pleased. And it struck me that telling what had happened was very important. I had told a story and that had mattered. I had become a storyteller in a way that I could never have imagined nor ever wanted. But since the killing happened in my parish, I went to the funeral to express my sympathy with the family of the victim. I wore a Roman collar and a black suit and walked into the cemetery past lines of uniformed Ulster Defence Regiment soldiers and stood beside the Church of Ireland clergy at the grave.

This public act offended members of the Unionist community, who tended to see priests as fellow travellers with the terrorists.

On the first week of March 1985, the *Impartial Reporter* carried a report of a debate in the Northern Ireland Assembly about security in the province, during which an elected representative from Fermanagh and member of the DUP, Rev. Ivan Foster, claimed that the Unionist population along the border had two enemies to contend with – the IRA who were killing their people, and the priests who tacitly supported them. The politician found it offensive to see a Catholic priest at the graves of dead Unionists, since the same clergy, he alleged, were so closely aligned to the IRA. Being at the funeral, he claimed, 'did not disassociate them from the murder'. And to illustrate his point he continued, 'I have a photograph of the priest from Derrylin, who not so long ago was shedding crocodile tears at the graveside of a UDR man … In this photograph, the priest is presenting medals to IRA men.'

Of course he was right. The men were in their nineties, the terrorist campaign he was speaking of was in the 1920s, and the medals had been presented to commemorate the centenary of the GAA the previous year.

Nevertheless, I was horrified and terrified. I was being painted as an IRA sympathiser, although nothing could have been further from the truth. I felt I was being publicly highlighted in a very sinister way. And I knew that there was a pattern at the time in Northern Ireland whereby certain politicians demonised individuals in public speeches over a sustained period of time until eventually some loyalist low-brained thug decided to do his duty and execute the person in question. So this was really serious stuff. I began to wake in the middle of the night in terror. And I was getting more scared each day.

The schoolteacher outside whose school the man had been killed wasn't too happy either, because one morning about a month after the shooting, a death threat was delivered to his classroom by telephone. The caller said he was a member of a particular paramilitary group, claimed he had committed a specific Belfast murder, had been involved in others and was 'not afraid to use a gun'. It crossed my mind that if the schoolteacher was at risk, then so was I. The RUC verified that the call had been valid and constituted a genuine threat and they offered the protection of armed police, who kept a close eye on us for a few weeks. Sometimes I would find their car parked in my backyard where the kittens had died.

Other people also advised us on security measures. I leaned a chair up against the hall door when I was going to bed each night. And I slept in one room but kept a light on in the room next door. Although that didn't convince me I would be safe if some yahoo came bursting down the hallway with a machine gun.

Most of all, I was horrified that by simply going to a funeral, crossing tribal lines to express my sympathy with a community who were victims of IRA violence and so show my disdain for murder, I myself could become a target. It was a raw example of Swift's observation that in Ireland we have just about enough religion to hate each other, but not enough to love. Like other leaders in the DUP, Rev. Ivan Foster was a ferocious defender of his people, but I felt his public comments were unfair and irresponsible and I wanted to do something about that. But I didn't know exactly what. Until I thought of Annaghmakerrig.

Bernard Loughlin was the director of the Tyrone Guthrie Centre. He created a standard of attention to detail in the organisation of the house that was remarkable – the cooking, the rituals of communal life, the cleaning of the dishwasher, the laying of flower gardens in the grounds. He expanded the vision of the centre, accommodating visual artists as well as writers, making more space available, converting old farm buildings into studios, examining artist retreats all over the world and bringing the best of international practice back to his beloved Annaghmakerrig. He had a vision of a different Ireland, a new, fresh, clean Ireland where art and literature were at the core of creating a cohesive society.

And so I arrived at his door one wet night in March, petrified with worry and anxiety, and copies of the *Impartial Reporter* under my arm. I told him what was going on in the local newspapers in Fermanagh, and what the local politician was implying about me.

'Let's have a look,' he said, and I showed him the

newspapers. He sat by the range in his socks, sipping a glass of Black Bush as he read. Then he looked at me.

'Well it's obvious what you're going to do,' he said.

'What am I going to do?' I wondered.

'Write back to him. You're a writer. Write him an open letter and give him a bit of your mind.'

And so I did. Bernard gave me the confidence I needed. He reminded me that a writer cannot be silent. That a writer must speak the truth, especially in difficult circumstances. And so I sat for hours at his table with pen and paper and in those hours I became a writer.

I stayed the night and drove back across the border in the morning and dropped the letter in the postbox in Derrylin. It was an open letter to Rev. Ivan Foster, and addressed to the Editor of the *Impartial Reporter*. It was published the following week. And that was the end of the matter.'

The schoolteacher wasn't so lucky. He was a quiet man to whom I sometimes chatted on Saturday mornings when we met in the shop. He was a gifted musician, though he was too shy to play in public. I used to cajole him about playing the organ in the church. I was going to start a choir, and do all the old-fashioned Latin bits for Easter, and we would buy a new electric keyboard if he agreed to play, and it would all be wonderful.

He agreed, somewhat reluctantly, but he came to me in late March before we had begun rehearsals to say he was pulling out. He had cancer. It was sudden and utterly

unexpected in a healthy man in his mid-fifties. On Good
Friday, the choir sang 'Stabat Mater' and a few other Latin
favourites without the new electric organ, which remained
in its box until the following month when it was brought
out and played for the first time at the schoolteacher's
funeral.

I believe the stress killed him. And it killed something
in me too. Or perhaps it allowed something very new to be
born. I had become a storyteller when I heard them shout
'Yahoo', and I had told that story. But now I had written
something that mattered and it had been published, and
that would make a difference. I had become a writer.

The dark-haired woman was far from my mind in
those months. I was alone in my terror. But in August she
phoned again. She had been in the Wicklow woods making
a sculpture all summer and she had just finished and was
chilling out and wanted to say hello. This time, her voice
wasn't on the answering machine. It was live. I was standing
in the hall with the phone shaking in my hand. But I was
ready for her.

'Come down,' I suggested. And she did, on the Omagh
bus. It was August 1985. We went down and looked at the
lake and wandered around Enniskillen and ate pizza in a
fancy restaurant and drank whiskey at the open fire in the
bungalow and slept in separate beds, as if we were both
unsure how to connect our unlikely romance the previous
year to this present moment in a priest's house.

On Monday morning, I drove her to the bus in Enniskillen. And when she was getting out of the car, as an afterthought she leaned over and kissed me on the cheek. Then we stared at each other and kissed lightly on the lips. A brief moment and it was gone. She was gone. I saw her in the back of the bus as it pulled away into the traffic. I drove back to Derrylin. I could do nothing for the rest of the day but think of her. I lay on the bed she had slept in, and wallowed in her scent still fresh on the pillow. I went to the church that evening and paced up and down the aisle, alone in a dark space, lit only by the red glow of the sanctuary lamp. *Oh God*, I thought, *if you are there, please help me*.

Suddenly I felt there was a presence other than mine in the building. As if someone was watching me. But it was not benign. Up on the balcony, I saw a shadow in the corner as if another person was standing there looking down at me. I even spoke out.

'Is there someone there?'

Because it just might have been a friend come to visit, who had seen the light on and slipped in to play a trick on me. Or it might have been a gunman come to kill me. Or perhaps it was Fr Fingers, at last, incarnate before my eyes. I went up the stairs and onto the balcony and there beside the organ was a long vertical pipe, which I had mistaken for the figure of a man. 'That's an end to you,' I said aloud. Because Fr Fingers was nothing more than a dark shadow in the remotest corner of my mind. And in the morning at 7 a.m., I phoned her. She was startled to get called so early.

'I've decided to go away,' I declared. 'Probably to Paris. I'm leaving here and I'm going away. And I was wondering, would you like to come?'

There was a pause.

'Why not Berlin?'

Anywhere, I thought to myself. *Just somewhere that's not here.* Because where I was, was nowhere.

So let's go. Pack the boxes. Clean out the presbytery. Phone a few friends and tell them it's over. Put the letter in the envelope and send it to the bishop. 'Dear Bishop, I'm off. This clerical life makes no sense to me. Goodbye.' Or words to that effect.

I got the loan of a Transit van and packed boxes of books into it, and my rocking chair and my stereo. I drove to Cavan where I dumped the lot in an unused bedroom in my mother's house.

'Where are you going?' she wanted to know.

'Dublin,' I said.

'Oh Jesus, Mary and St Joseph,' she said.

'That's right,' I said.

From Cavan, I cycled ten miles to a crossroads on the Dublin road and waited for a bus. I could have taken the bus from Cavan, but I was too proud. I'd sold the Datsun to make a few pounds, and I was too ashamed to be seen standing on the street in Cavan waiting for a bus. Someone might say, look at him, he left the priesthood and now he's waiting for a bus, the poor bastard.

Dublin was different because I was anonymous. It was a dry, crisp autumn and I cycled around with glee and abandon, as motorists tensed their fists around the steering wheels as I came at them, wobbling and unruly, in the urban traffic.

The dark-haired woman had a life in Dublin. A son. A home. A studio. And a reputation as an artist. I loved being at her side, though I got into arguments with her friends who would corner me in the kitchenettes of various apartments during parties and interrogate me. I would say I was a writer but eventually someone would ask too many questions and I would admit what I had been and they would say, 'Oh, so you're one of those sleazy bastards.'

We didn't go to Paris or Berlin, but the following year we spent a summer together in Italy. It was a kind of fake elopement. I wanted to get away from people who reminded me that I had been a priest, and she wanted to take her son on a holiday.

Not that I was going to get very far away from Catholicism in Subiaco, a town east of Rome in a ridge of mountains where St Benedict had lived in a cave in the sixth century. A monastery still leans over the cliff. I fell in love with the town the moment I got off the bus. I traipsed around all afternoon, wondering where everyone was because I was unused to the habit of taking a siesta. The town was a silent maze of sloped streets that burst into life around 4.30 p.m. The shutters opened on pizza parlours, fashion shops, cafés, trattorias and small grocery stores, and boys in white shirts floated up and down the cobbled streets on sparkling chrome motorbikes, and girls in blue denim with tanned shoulders dangled their feet from the little walls as they ate ice-creams.

I cooled the palms of my hands on a glass of Coke and felt dizzy, even with the shade of an umbrella that sheltered my table outside a birreria. An elderly waiter pitied me. He had a black dicky bow and neatly combed grey hair, and his face was cobweb purple. He struggled for breath as he smoked, and he said something to me in Italian.

'I'm Irish,' I replied.

'Ah, Bobby Sands.'

'Yes,' I said, 'Bobby Sands.'

He brought me a Coke and didn't charge me and I sipped it for twenty minutes until my new landlord arrived.

Fabiano was in his sixties. He wore a white linen suit, white shoes, a black T-shirt and dark glasses. But he looked like he'd just got out of bed. His hair was black and his face was red. He was bloodshot and bleary-eyed. He had a brief word with the waiter, lit a cigarette and brought his espresso over to my table, his white jacket now slung over his left shoulder and the sunglasses on his head.

I flung my rucksack into the back of his car and he drove me to a three-storey villa on the edge of town just above the main road. Fabiano lived alone on the top floor. His son and daughter-in-law occupied the middle floor with their two children, which was ideal since the artist would be arriving two weeks later with her son, who was about the same age, and on the ground level there was a two-roomed apartment which opened onto a terrace of stone flags with white seats, and all around was a garden of weeping willow trees and yellow shrubs and borders of blazing red flowers. In the centre, a swing seat lay idle beneath a willow tree. In the evenings Fabiano would sit there, watching his grandchildren play bowls in the distance, listening to his son and daughter-in-law chatting on their balcony, and watching me through darkly tinted spectacles. I joined him one evening and he told me that he had built the house and garden for his wife. It was to be their pleasure in retirement.

'All my life I sell the fruit,' he said. 'This was to be *paradiso*.'

But his wife had died the year the house was finished, so

she never enjoyed the garden they had dreamed about for years as they sold melons on the streets of Rome.

The day before the artist and her eleven-year-old son arrived, I scrubbed the floor and laid out a feast of wines and salami and cheese and pasta and salad on the kitchen table. Then at seven o'clock in the morning, I boarded a blue bus at the foot of the garden for Rome.

Outside Termini train station, I paced for an hour, admiring the gypsies in long skirts as they danced and flitted through the crowd, begging and selling holy pictures. Then her hand touched my shoulder and I knew her immediately. I turned around and there she was, radiant in the brilliant sunshine, laughing and hugging me with expressive enthusiasm that neither of us would have indulged in at home in the Irish rain where only ambiguous emotions are valid. I wore a white shirt and trousers. My hair was cut tight to my skull. My face was red from the sun but her skin was as tan as a chestnut.

'The weather in Ireland has been great,' she said, 'and I was carving all month, up in Wicklow. But it will take me time to get used to this heat.' She wiped her brow and we went into the waiting room where her young son was minding the suitcases. Later, on the bus, as the boy stared out the window with uncertain curiosity, she put her hand in mine.

'Take off the cardigan,' I said. And she did. And then she smiled and said, 'That's better,' and we kissed and sat back and began to enjoy the adventure as the boy beside us blushed with embarrassment.

The bus brought us through deep gorges and along cliffs and slopes and to the ledge of deep ravines, and we looked out the window and were amazed, and silent, and we stole glances at each other like teenagers.

Her son endured the awkward world wherein his mother, already divorced, was now testing the possibility of life with another man, while he fended for himself on the streets or played ball with other children whose language he did not understand.

At night when the boy slept, we drank Frascati by candlelight, our faces floating in the darkness beside the flames, like figures in ancient paintings. The window was always open. The salad bowl was dotted with black olives. The noise of insects in the garden outside the window encouraged us to make love. We stayed in our room for hours with the shutters down, straddling each other, transfixed, amazed and relaxed. Sometimes we committed the act with the embarrassment of strangers, and sometimes with the guilt of teenagers. With the shame of plunderers or like empty beings on a train to nowhere who just needed each other for a moment. We both had separate fantasies and at times we were strangers to each other. And always when we had finished, and the passion had subsided and we had washed and I knew it was over for another day, there grew in me a kind of relief, that our moment of intensity had

73

been conducted with competence and without a hitch and I could go back to exploring the town or the garden or the hills around us or just drink more wine.

When other people chatted on the two balconies above us or when the children played in the garden, we stole away from the world and closed the shutters and the door. We were unlocking some frozen core in our souls, healing each other from previous lives, from past mistakes and from childhood sorrow. We were growing younger, or at least understanding that even for the broken it is possible to play at being children again. And then we returned to the table and finished the fruit and the cream and strawberry sponge and experimented with the coffee maker.

I watched her dress in the mornings. I lay as a child might lie, content with a loving mother. In the heat of Italy, her body merged with all the women on the street, and her scent mingled with a hundred other perfumes in the air. Her wardrobe filled with small things from elegant shops in the town. I was in heaven. And yet the pleasure was unbearable.

We walked to Jenne one morning, all three of us, a village of red-tiled roofs over ten miles away. We walked on small mountain roads, the morning sun burning off the mist in the valleys below. We walked in short trousers, T-shirts and white runners. Our clothes drenched with sweat. After what seemed like a long time, we arrived in the village and guzzled cool beers and Coca-Cola in the shade of a shop while the village slept. We came home on a dusty country bus with old people who had weather-beaten faces. We had wine and cold pasta from the fridge and the boy went to the garden to play and we lay on the bed ready again for the conversation our bodies held in secret beyond where words reached. And as the cicadas sang in the night, we sat on the veranda with candles and maps, planning where we might walk the following day.

We went to Campo dell'Osso and dined in a mountain restaurant. The old waiter was fat and wore a white apron, and a woman with a bonnet on her head looked out from the kitchen now and again to see if the customers were eating well. There was an open fire in the centre of the room on raised bricks and an oven above the flames from which the fat waiter shovelled warm loaves of bread for our minestrone. When the spaghetti came, we used the warm bread to mop up the creamy mushroom and pepper sauce. We even asked for second helpings and laughed at each new Italian word we learned as we ate without knives or forks. And we had a second bottle of wine. And we came home on a village bus. And there was three of us: me, the woman and her child. But when the night enveloped us, we went alone to our room and we went down again into private places of wound and shame where our bodies strived for healing in unconscious acts of erotic love. It could not have been more perfect. More complete. Everyone was happy. The children were sleeping. Their parents were sitting on balconies. Fabiano beneath his willow was swinging on the swinging seat.

Yet each morning, I would walk around the garden smoking and feeling uneasy.

Men, they say, rarely cry – but I cry a lot. Watching romantic movies or listening to certain pieces of music. But I never cried as much as when I made love. Not that she could see the tears. They were inside and invisible. But no less real that the orgasm. And it was in that same moment, in the height of ecstasy and just a little beyond it, I felt as if my body was being squeezed of a great flood of tears, and a sense of sorrow oozed from every pore. When I climaxed, I cried deeply inside and felt unspeakable unease, and knew not why.

It's a dizzy height to be at, up there, fully climaxed, so full of juice and potency. And then to be released. But inside me in that moment, when the immediate bliss had just about passed, there came the most withering of all sensations – a loneliness that was private and which seemed like the most uneasy of all sins. In some undefined way, love was a betrayal of myself. A closing down of an inner voice, some clock ticking in the dark interior that I was refusing to heed. When the ecstasy was over, I felt alone and guilty each time. Not on account of having made love, but on account of having heard such a deeply solitary music on the inside and having not been capable of sharing it. That was the most sorrowful thing in the world, and though we smiled at each other and though I would say truthfully that our moment of sexual union had been exquisite, there was something else undeclared.

After a month, we took a bus to a remote fortress of stone walls in the clouds of heaven. A village so high up that the only way in was on foot, where no car engine disturbed the quiet of the cobbled streets in the afternoon siesta. I wanted to seal our elopement, our fake honeymoon, in that world of white matrimonial sheets that flapped on one hundred clotheslines criss-crossing the narrow lanes. The village's mediaeval stones would give me the courage to seal our future not just with a kiss but with a promise. I would say something beautiful. I would say, 'Will you marry me?' and she would say 'Yes.' And the future would fall into place.

We stayed overnight in the mountain refuge with a piss pot in the closet which I used three times, and which made the artist laugh each time she heard the water pass at a hot spurting pelt into the bottom of the chamber pot. And she whispered in my ear when I got back into bed, and soon she was asleep, but I never found the moment to say the right thing.

I had been in Italy for almost three months, but time was running out. One Saturday morning in mid-July, we were lying in bed. She was stretched on her back and I was curled in a ball around her. We were letting time pass, when in the distance we heard voices. Very far away. It sounded like a choir. Or the chorus of an opera. And it got closer and louder.

We went out onto the terrace and looked over the railings and saw a procession of men and women in farming clothes and hiking gear moving along the road. Some of the women wore black dresses and mantillas. Everyone walked with a stick and a picnic, wrapped in a scarf or in a plastic bag, as they moved along in a snake-like procession around the winding roads, singing hymns whose melodies were familiar to me and made me cry. It took an hour for the procession to meander around the farthest corner and out of sight as they headed towards the Aniene River and the road that would take them to the Cave of the Holy Trinity in the hills above.

That was the day everything changed. I stood on the balcony for a long time after they were gone and she went into the bedroom and slept. Something in their faithful peasant faces called out to me. Reminded me of the exquisite ecstasy to be found in solitude and prayer, and I was overwhelmed with guilt.

After that, the emphasis of our adventures changed. We did less drinking. More walking. And our walking was leading more and more in the one direction. We went to visit the nearby monastery of St Benedict. We were greeted at a big wooden door by an old blind monk with white hair and dead eyes hidden by sunglasses. He introduced himself as Fr Ambrose and he could point to all the frescos on the walls and describe the images with complete accuracy, despite his blindness. He showed us bullet holes in the window frame behind the altar, caused by Allied troops on their march northwards during the Second World War. He put his finger in gaping holes in the altar as if he were fingering the wounds of Christ himself. He rubbed the palm of his hand on the frescos as if he were touching his own mother. I lingered in the gift shop looking at rosary beads. The artist kept her distance. At the great wooden door to the outside world, I thanked the monk and shook his hand.

'Actually, I'm a priest,' I said, puffed up with pride.

She looked at me as if I had betrayed her.

That evening Fabiano came to our window, as he often did, with a basket of fruit. On this occasion he had a bunch of flowers for the artist. She took them and thanked him and started to cry. Fabiano was startled but he read the situation quickly enough, and seemed very disappointed as he withdrew from the room.

79

The rest was inevitable. I left a few days later, heading alone on the blue bus to Rome and back to Dublin with Aer Lingus, while she and her son went north to spend time with friends near Lake Como and, I suppose, to allow her wounds to heal.

In the years that followed Subiaco, I worked hard as a writer, producing plays and books, and she got on with her life in her studio in Temple Bar and her son grew up and went to art college. We met to drink, talk, watch movies or make love, but I always retained my own space in Cowper Street or Sandycove, while she lived in Dundrum. Sometimes I would move into her apartment for a few weeks or months, but it never seemed to work because I couldn't fit in to an existing family unit. Sometimes I would vanish altogether for a few months, to Donegal or Clare, and all that time I drank a lot in Grogans or The Norseman, and was often angry and argumentative. When I got drunk, I went wild. I'd stand on anyone's table at three in the morning and take my clothes off if the music suited, or argue with anyone I could find until they were blue in the face. The hangovers were atrocious, and bleak.

Inside me there was a hidden grief. It had no form or shape or cause. Yet it permeated everything I did. And I felt shame, not just about being a priest, but about being a man. My masculinity had disintegrated. Feelings of kinship and sonship and belonging in the universe were withered. And when all that collapsed, there was a price to pay. For me, the world became the empty existential wilderness I had read about in Eliot, Camus and Nietzsche. And I wasn't alone in this grief. I could see the same despair all around me, in the faces of other men at every street corner, those without jobs or meaning, or in the faces of old bachelors on farms in Cavan gone to ruin and wild. The insights of genius had apparently percolated down to the most inarticulate mind in the bar, and all men were losers. The message was

80

getting clearer as my world became peopled more and more by drunks, staring at the television screens in speechless bewilderment. And every young boy was depressed, full of foggy intimations of impending doom, or was transfixed by grief that sometimes left them hanging on the end of a rope, or wandering the outskirts of various towns and villages in slow motion, like zombies on antidepressants. What made us men was no longer any good.

But I had a way out of it. Because if there was one thing that made me feel alive, it was being in love. That was my salvation. That was the thing that made everything else coherent. Love made meaning of the world. Everything belonged and was bright when love sat at the centre. And my centre was the woman with the dark hair; as long as I clung to her, I would be safe. So for seven years in Dublin, I clung to her, though we lived only a kind of uncommitted half-life together. The kind of accommodation that suits Ireland, where you take the bits you can and don't bother changing the rest. And yet there was something between us that I couldn't let go of. So I persisted, and finally I succeeded.

Seven years later, the artist became the beloved, officially, in a village in east Galway called Shekana. My mother came to the wedding. And a few friends and relations, and lots of people whom the artist had known in Dublin. She wore a simple willow-green suit and she held flowers in her hand. We stood in the church porch as April sunlight hit the tiles at our feet. I remember seeing my mother standing alone in the car park, slim and graceful in her seventies. She walked over to us in the porch and wished us luck, and then nodded in consternation when she saw my new wife's tall and handsome son standing beside us. 'You never told me she had children,' she whispered to me in horror.

There was a lot I hadn't told my mother. Cathy Carman was a distinguished sculptor. She had a studio in Temple Bar and had exhibited in group shows and solo shows over a number of years and was highly regarded for her figurative work in bronze, stone and wood. But when Temple Bar was targeted for development, many of the artists fled, no longer able to enjoy the silence of derelict streets in the centre of the city, and no longer able to afford studios in what was becoming a commercial zone. So she was interested in moving down the country. It might be a new adventure.

Her son had finished art college and was working in a bronze-casting foundry. We were both just reaching forty, and still young enough to imagine we might be able to build a new future together. But I was marrying an artist who was as penniless as myself. And we were moving to a remote farmhouse on the Leitrim border, not just because Leitrim was a fashionable haven for artists at the time but because it was about the only place artists could afford to live.

We didn't have a hotel reception after the wedding ceremony. We had rented a two-storey farmhouse near the village of Keadue as our new home, and it hummed all night with music and dancing. There was a wedding cake which we cut in pieces on the wall outside the house, as everyone gathered around just as the light was failing, and we lit candles and made speeches, and we laughed. When the guests had all gone home, we cleaned up and went to a musty bed upstairs, as the morning came and the room filled with grey light. I hoped it might be the beginning of a new dawn for me.

Thirteen litres of red wine were left over from the party, so we spent a few weeks sleeping and drinking, surrounded by birch trees, foxes and badgers. The cuckoo was late that year. We waited each day for him but there was no sign. We hardly got out of bed, and we thanked the rain because it rained every day and all night, and the sound of it on the roof was delicious. It held our attention and blessed us. We knew we were alone in the world, except for the pheasants. In the daytime, the rain continued. We were in harmony and there was no surveillance. Neither parent nor child, policeman nor priest could spy on us. Just the two of us, silent and alone and hardly able to stop making love. Neither daughter nor mother, uncle nor cousin to bother us. No friends or brothers. No stranger or enemy. And God was off duty. God was an old-fashioned idea. There were only the pheasants and us. And we both licked it up, and fucked and slept and woke and laughed. And then laughed more.

Our daughter was born in February. There was a deep snow on the roads and in the fields when we drove home

83

from the hospital with her bundled fresh body in the back seat. I opened the window of the bedroom one day and handed in a bunch of daffodils, as the beloved kept a blanket over the baby's head for fear of a chill wind. By May, the child had grown big and plump and the house we were renting had a cracked chimney and smoke seeped into the upstairs rooms. *What would we do in winter?* I wondered, when we would need fires every evening and the baby would be sleeping in her cot upstairs.

In July we found a small cottage for sale in the hills above Lough Allen and, with a loan from the bank because no one would give us a mortgage, we bought it. And we bought a fridge and linoleum for the kitchen and the child grew strong as an ox on my knee beside the range. Sometimes she would try to get matches from my breast pocket and rattle them, as I tried to smoke cigarettes. So I decided to stop smoking. And then I went off the drink and started planting trees. I planted rows of beech saplings and oak and alder and birch and my hands shook as I planted each one, and I wept buckets of tears out there in the field where no one could see me and where the rain wiped them all away.

'Is there something you're not telling me?' the beloved asked.

There was. There was something I wasn't telling anyone, because I had not yet admitted it to myself.

The word 'depression' makes me think of bewildered strangers in far-off wheelchairs or feeble old men staring at the wall in nursing homes or lying in bed with the curtains closed. People twitching on buses or swatting imaginary flies. I saw depressed people consuming antidepressants like Smarties throughout their meaningless days, as they walked the roads around the town in slow motion, numb to joy or the loveliness of trees. I knew many people who walked in slow motion about the town but I never stopped to say hello. They had already moved beyond this world. They were separated from ordinary life as if by a wall of glass. As far as I was concerned, they were walking dead. And like the remoteness of old age to a young man, their condition didn't seem to have any relevance to me.

But as the trees grew in the garden and the child began watching Barney the purple dinosaur on television in the afternoons, I began to feel sluggish. I was in my forties. I had written six plays for the Abbey Theatre and published two novels, so in some sense I was a successful writer. But the money garnished from full-time writing barely put bread on the table. It barely paid the interest on the overdraft or covered the heating costs for the tiny cottage we had bought in 1994. And now I was slowing down. It seemed at times that the country was awash with money. There were houses going up everywhere, arts centres being opened in every big town, and a general air of well-being infected the arts community. But it didn't reach me. I was just getting older. Sometimes things would go so still that I would find myself transfixed in a chair, just staring out the window or gazing into the fire. I felt locked in. Almost unable to shake the still air and move, until someone walked into the room and interrogated me.

'What are you doing there?' they would ask.

'Nothing.'

Because I was thinking of nothing. I was in a state of transfixed emptiness. I no longer thought about what to get for the dinner or how to clean the room or where to put my socks. I was wallowing in remorse. I should have fucked more women when I was in my twenties, I told myself, instead of getting dragged into the melancholic cloisters of a seminary. I should have travelled abroad instead of trying to grow trees in Leitrim where only rushes grow. Around me I saw only the debris of a life destroyed. And it all came to a head in the dry hot summer of 1995.

I broke a hole in the wall of the coal shed and put in a window. I made a floor and ceiling of timber beams. I made a door from planks of pine. And when the walls were painted peach white, and the timbers warmed with Oregon Rosewood stain, everyone agreed that the coal shed no longer existed. It was gone, and in its stead was a pure empty space, clean and cool, and because of the absence of electricity and the predominance of timber, it had a mediaeval feel to it. Each day I would steal into the empty room. There wasn't a breath of air outside. The sun was a ball of fire in the clear blue sky. I would sit in the dead heat of the afternoon, on the bare floor, silent and still. The window faced north. I listened to the flies and the bees in the garden and dreamed about the south of France and a woman I once knew who lived there.

Some people come into our lives like guardians from other worlds. It is as if they were sent to watch over us, to give us some indefinable sustenance on our journey. The sort of person you never get to know well. You never get close to them. You only meet them occasionally every few years and yet their presence is enduring and continuous, and significant in the deepest recesses of the heart. Sabine was that kind of person. I first met her in the mid-1970s, in Grogans pub, near Grafton Street in Dublin. She had arrived from Paris and she had found work as a model in the College of Art in Dún Laoghaire, and she lived in a small flat with two Irish girls. She learned English from them and soon the three were inseparable. Their humour, laughter and kindness flowed as one stream. The men who hung around them usually craved money, drugs or sex, but being in the women's company was like a healing process for everyone. It was as if all the craving had been suspended for a few hours. As if everything had ceased except their laughter. And I always felt Sabine to be the heart of this odd and wonderful nexus. I remember her big woolly jumpers, the incense sticks, the candlelight, the soft French vowels, musical as a blackbird and as clear as a bell in the dead of night. When she left Ireland suddenly, the centre fell apart and I lost contact with the others.

But four years later, I tried a phone number in Paris and got lucky, and we agreed to meet outside the Pompidou Centre where she was distributing anti-nuclear leaflets. I had been ordained a priest the previous month.

A classmate of mine, John O'Donohue, had been ordained the same week. When all the celebrations were over, we slipped off to Europe for a holiday. We travelled overland in a truck. John Finlay, the driver, was a cousin of mine. We crossed the Alps near Mont Blanc and descended on a steep zigzag road into Italy and on to Milan. We parted with my cousin, a six-foot-tall wild Irishman, in a bar called The Toby Jug, and went by train to Venice and stayed for a short while in a monastery on the Lido, scouring the city during the day for art and music. After a few weeks we got bored with each other and decided to split up. John opted for Florence to imbibe more culture and I went north into the Dolomite mountains in search of romantic adventures. I came home by Milan, taking a lift with another Irish truck driver from Monaghan, who brought me as far as Paris, where I found Sabine.

We spent a few days together. Visited Nôtre Dame. Had a meal one evening in a Turkish restaurant. But mostly we hung out for hours on the street, with the anti-nuclear leaflets and a tin whistle. When she put her arms around me at the train station to bid farewell, I felt the strength of her body through her woollen jumper, and I sensed how tightly we both might have clung to each other in another life. The intensity of it left me dizzy all the way to London, regretting, even after four weeks, that I had been ordained a priest.

And that was the end of it. Until I had come to the end of my time in Derrylin. I had the bags packed and the books in boxes. It was my last day in the priesthood. A letter came through the door. It contained small notebook-size pages,

89

saffron in colour and written with a biro. Sabine wrote that she had entered a contemplative convent in the south of France and that in its enclosed space, in its great silence, in its strict old-world regime, she had found a peace that she had never known in the world.

We were going in opposite directions and that made me slightly uneasy, but I folded the tiny pages neatly back in the envelope and placed them in my back pocket, where by chance they remained until the day I finished painting the coal shed ten years later. I was wearing the old ragged trousers for the painting job, and the letter fell out of the back pocket just as I finished. I opened the little saffron pages and read them over and over again. And I took them to be a sign.

OK, I'd been married for a few years. I had a wonderful partner and daughter and I was happy on the outside. In a few short years, I had learned all about bottles and feeds and teething and how babies talk. My most recent play, *Hubert Murray's Widow*, had been a moderate success in the Peacock Theatre and I was beginning to write a new one. But I was forty-two and, on the inside, I was empty again.

Something still called to me in the dark of night and woke me from sleep. A clock was still ticking in the distance. And no matter how busy I was with the baby or my partner or writing for theatre, some inner space inside me still felt like a black hole, because since I had left the priesthood I had missed the consolation of faith.

The country was beginning to reel from daily revelations of child abuse by priests. Catholic Ireland was dying on the television every night, and yet there was something in the secular world that made me uncomfortable. Its coldness, its indifference disturbed me. It was much easier to retreat to the womb and believe that the universe was like a mother, all around me, enfolding me, and minding me in every breath I drew.

So I decided that the coal shed was going to become a little meditation room, a place of refuge just for me. A place where I could hide from the world and try to make it back to an earlier time. I would recover the innocence of faith again in the privacy of that little building. I would examine what I had lost and, like a nun in her cloister, I would rekindle my faith with a few candles and an icon of the Virgin Mary. I would put the broken vessel together again. I would live again in the joyful hope of a heavenly kingdom. And towards all this, Sabine's letter was like a road map. It just fell out of my pocket and pointed the way. I had no doubt that the scrawls of ink on the faded pages were a wonderful message from a guardian angel.

But there is no going back in life. And I did not find a way to pray again. On the contrary, the hours I spent in the empty room were a time of lament and of letting go. A time of closure and saying goodbye.

I became a priest in 1981. Four years later I walked away and it took me years to come to terms with it. Moving

91

on in normal life is a lonely business, but moving away from the icons of one's religious faith is devastating. And yet finally it must be done. I needed to say goodbye to all the hocus-pocus. I was fatherless in the world.

Yet even now I am still haunted by my father's ghost. His sterility. His short life. His face in the mirror. His pain in death.

I remember how he lay in a bed with cot sides in a Cavan hospital. He had spent months in hospital being investigated for chronic pain in his back, but the doctors never came up with any satisfactory result and, in the end, he became physically exhausted. He was in his seventies. I was twenty-one, and I knew he was dying.

His body had shrivelled to a skeleton. The bedsores were as large as golf balls. One Saturday afternoon, I shook his hand, his long white bony hand, and I said goodbye. Actually I said I was going back to the mountains of west Cavan where I lived at that time because, as I explained to him, I had an appointment with a hairdresser. I recall his long, slender white arm. His jagged elbow. The slow care with which he folded the limb back in under the white sheet, as if the linen or the starch would hurt his skin. He was smiling. I remember him always smiling. And he made a joke. Something about taking care on the road. I tried to speak, but he took his hand again from under the sheet and this time he placed his finger to his lips in a gesture commanding silence. He pointed up into the air again.

And smiled. As if to indicate a presence other than ours in the room.

'Shhh,' he whispered. 'The man above!'

I nodded.

'Yes,' I agreed. 'The man above.'

He was bidding farewell. Later that day, I was in a friend's house in Glangevlin, sitting on a hard kitchen chair as a young girl cut my hair. The phone rang. It was an old manual phone in the hallway. You could imagine the postmistress down in the village winding some knob as it rang out in long extended bells. The girl answered it as I sat ignoble in the middle of her kitchen. A towel around my shoulders, my hair scattered on the floor.

'The hospital wants to speak with you,' she said in a solemn tone of foreboding.

He was almost fifty when he had married in 1950. He had fathered two sons. In retirement he would lie on the bed upstairs, in the semi-detached house he had bought with my mother in 1952, and he would listen to the BBC on a transistor set my brother brought him from America, and which he never ceased to marvel at. He listened to news programmes. And sometimes he would come downstairs and listen to *The Mikado* on his hi-fidelity record player. His black box. He often walked the roads that wind around the drumlins in Cavan and he drank bottles of stout in the evenings. One bottle each evening, with his arse to the fire and a cigarette in his hand. A ritual that transported him

93

from the mundane world of his work as an accountant in the local authority to the more sublime world of home, his books, his armchair and his endless reflections on the nature of the universe and the possibility of God. He could talk theology all night, but conversation was hard to find in a small rural town in the 1950s. For him, the clergy lacked intellectual finesse. He had no family. His only sister had died during the First World War. His granny was Polish. He remembered the Easter Rising in Dublin, where he spent his youth playing in the rubble. His Polish roots remain a mystery and the stories are now lost in history. I didn't interrogate him enough when he was alive, and I only loved him from the day he died.

The year after his death, in 1977, I returned to Maynooth as a student. I was twenty-four, and was beginning a course in theology that would lead me to ordination. Even then, it did not escape my notice that there was a connection between my father's death and my decision to study for the priesthood.

It was an exciting time in the Church. People were trying to make a clean start after the Second Vatican Council. The pomp and circumstance of papal power had been taken away, so that the simple truth of the gospel could live and be lived in a fuller way. A preferential option for the poor! A commitment to the margins!

And in that mood of renewal, I began a four-year journey towards ordination. We studied the writings of

Leonardo Boff, Hans Küng, Edward Schillebeeckx, Juan Luis Segundo, Gustavo Gutiérrez and Charles Curran, and many more I have forgotten. Everything was going great. Until the pope died.

I thought of Pope Paul VI as a cross between Hamlet and Danny la Rue. He was liberal, uncertain and effeminate in his manners. Even in old age, there was something beguiling about the genteel grace in his smile, the white silk robes, the delicate air of mediaeval papal drag in his carriage. I imagined him reading Camus and Sartre, crying in his drinking chocolate and being riddled with uncertainties. When the cardinals elected a new guy with a big smile, who reminded me of the actor Anthony Quinn, everything seemed as it should be in the grand design of history. Water cannot flow uphill. A clock can never be turned back. And nobody can put history into reverse.

But the poor old pope was drinking his drinking chocolate one night, or perhaps it was soup or tea (the world may never know the true details), when something didn't agree with him. Either the drinking chocolate or some terrible idea in his mind or the future of planet earth or just the clammy burden of being a pope squeezed the fat of his heart to an unbearable rigour. The cup dropped from his hand and the nun who popped her head in to see if he was all right some hours later realised when she spoke to him that the silence in his ears would never be broken again by another papal bull.

95

There was a lot of speculation about how he died. But there's nothing as dead as a dead pope, so in a matter of weeks he was sealed in lead and buried under stone, and the cardinal archbishops of the Church got down to work once more. Another game of blindfold chess with the Holy Spirit behind closed doors. And thus came Karol Wojtyla to the throne of St Peter.

Little did we know then that in the decade that followed, every theologian we had studied would be either thrown out of the Church or declared heretical. Their books banished from the shelves of seminaries around the world. Little did we know that Karol Wojtyla would restore a formidable code of canon law, promulgate a new catechism, and reinstate a solid sense of hierarchy, authority and centralisation in the management of the Church. Little did anyone imagine that time and the Roman Curia would fatally wound the ideals of collegiality, community and openness that had marked the aftermath of the Second Vatican Council.

From the day that Karol Wojtyla became pope, I could feel something had changed. I could definitely sense something different in the Maynooth air. Things felt different. The cloisters looked the same. The books on the shelves were the same. But when I looked closely at the gaunt intellectuals among my classmates, the liberals who walked with their chins out ahead of them, the ones I always watched like a barometer to gauge the colour of the political sky, I could sense trouble. No. I could sense despair. People who had read more theology than me, and who were – up to that leafy autumn day – crystal clear about the kind of liberal Church that was going to emerge in the future, suddenly seemed as if they had all been run over by a bus. They carried themselves around in a daze.

One year later, the new pope came to Ireland. The long hand of Rome reaching deep into our little dreams and hopes. His voice, soft as a radio announcer – a warm mahogany voice when he had a good microphone – became harsh in the loudspeakers around the Phoenix Park. The pope even made arrangements to drop in to Maynooth to pay us all a personal visit, though there were those of us who wished he would stay away. Some of us looked at the mist covering the tip of the spire above the main chapel, which Sean O'Casey once called a spike through the heart of the Irish people, and hoped the mist would come lower so that the helicopter would, like the Angel of Exodus, pass us by and head off somewhere else. But the mist lifted. The power of God revealed itself in the chopper's blades! And the long arm of Rome became a flock of shadows moving along the corridors.

In some ways, the papal visit was the funeral of Catholicism in Ireland. After the cheers of the assembled millions had died away and the sick and infirm who had waited too long in the drizzle at Knock had been returned to their homes and hospitals and hospices, Irish society found that it couldn't really stomach the harsh tone of

97

Rome's teachings and bit by bit went off to gorge and be lost in a frenzy of secular self-improvement. Those who stayed within the Church grew more and more to love the voice of his clear authority, and the strong protective arm of the Good Shepherd who could ring-fence the mind and heart against all ambiguities or uncertainties that were festering in the lost world. A world of depraved ideas and tendencies.

And of course there was no depravity within the Church. Or at least if there was, it was of the utmost importance to hide it. The rest, as they say, is history.

Many years later, I watched the pope die before my eyes on television. It was an astonishing event. His last struggle to bless and to speak at the window. His mighty heart. His simple coffin. And it seemed as if a generation of young people were flocking to Rome like a mediaeval pilgrimage, to be close to the dying priest. In this great warrior-death, with the aid of television and the co-operation of the pope himself, a new generation was brought through the slow unfolding of grief in a simple and natural death-watch.

And I too waited. I watched the window for any movement in the curtains. Any significance in the changing of lights as the days passed. Rome filled up with young people and still I waited. Europe was on the move. CNN and BBC News didn't let up. The world was being called to attention.

It was a death that typified the man. He had a lesson to

98

teach, about the dignity of suffering – perhaps about the inevitability of suffering – and to that end he controlled and orchestrated it all. As much as he possibly could, he arranged everything. His dying and death became a ritual that illustrated a profound lesson on the nobility and necessity of human suffering. Or so he hoped.

And this was a man in control. A man who was not frightened or helpless in a fog of confusion as he moved towards his last breath, but a man with one eye firmly on the Day of Resurrection and the other on the crowd, that they too would see what he saw and hear what he heard, and hopefully die like he died.

I sat up all night. I couldn't take my eyes off the television. I felt a sense of awe about his stature. His authority. His clear teachings. His unrelenting love and support for human life in all its forms and stages and situations. He had kept intact the glory of Christ's teachings. You couldn't deny that. A seamless logic, which can be passed on to the next generation as a staff to walk with and a lamp to guide them. We may have been burying the pope, but the pope was well and truly burying any last remnant of liberality in this complete pageant of his dying.

I was amazed at how much his life had shaped mine. I was twenty-six years old when he became pope. And, with the rest of the world, I lived twenty-six years in the shadow of his colossal vision. Like many others whose faith was often a tentative glimmer of light in the vast night of darkness, he shaped us by banishing us. He left no room at the table for those who disagreed. He showed us the door and told us to choose.

But I am also grateful that his life and authority forced me to rethink my vocation as a priest. Forced me to walk in the wilderness. To make sense of my life in a different way; as a storyteller and playwright and lover.

When I think of my father, and his skeletal hand blessing me from his deathbed, I hope now that I have not failed him. I know that his hand was telling me that it was OK, no matter what I did. His fragility was his unconditional love. His yes to everything. His ease with uncertainty. His comic blindfold dance over the cliff. His lack of a strategy when he became terminally ill. His soft falling backwards into the abyss, to be engulfed by the swell of death rising like an ocean in his withered body.

But when I think of Pope John Paul II, I think of his strength and clarity, his face like a rock carved into love, and I am shaken with humility. But I am also frightened. Because I could not live up to his expectations. I failed the pope.

Like almost everyone in Ireland in the mid-1990s, I had become sickened by the endless revelations of clerical child abuse and the ways in which Church leaders had hidden the truth for decades. It made me truly ashamed of the fact that I had once been a priest. It seemed like nothing good could be said about the clerical institutions of the Catholic Church. Even my mother, who was then eighty years of age, seemed quietly disillusioned with the Church. We usually went to visit her once a week as a family – me, the wife and the child. And she delighted in having a daughter-in-law and a grandchild and any misgivings she ever had about me leaving the priesthood were clearly dispelled.

The coal shed was never converted into a Christian oratory. Instead, I used it as a tiny writing studio, though there was barely enough room for a small table and chair, and there was no electricity. I used an extension cable from the house to power an electric typewriter which sat on the table and I sat on the chair wearing a large overcoat and a woollen hat, and began writing the first draft of a play that eventually became *Sour Grapes* and was produced at the Peacock Theatre in 1997. It was the third and final play in a trilogy about the collapsing Church. The first was *Una Pooka*, a black comedy about Pope John Paul II's visit to Ireland, followed by *Misogynist*, an experimental multimedia work, which was presented on the Abbey Theatre's main stage at the Dublin Theatre Festival in 1991. Now I was finishing off the trilogy, writing a kind of epilogue for a Church in disgrace.

But I wasn't quite done with magical thinking. Just when I had made my way out of one religion, I found myself drawn to another. One day I was driving back from Cavan alone after a visit to my mother and I was just a few miles outside Ballinamore when I saw a sign on the side of the road. Jampa Ling. Strange words that seemed out of place in the middle of Leitrim. I turned off the main road and about three miles down the boreen I came to the gates of an old mansion on the left-hand side. I drove up an avenue of potholes, sheltered by huge larch trees, and arrived at a gravel parking area outside an elegant nineteenth-century house. It was midsummer. There were prayer flags hanging like bunting between two ancient oak trees.

Inside, a group of young people, mostly women, were preparing for evening prayers. They had gathered in the Shrine Room, or what used to be the old drawing room of the house. The walls were painted red and gold. And the room was cluttered with Buddhist icons and fresh flowers. Everyone prostrated three times towards the Buddha. Then they sat in lotus or Zen positions. I leaned against the back wall and closed my eyes, allowing the sound of the chants and chiming bells to flow over me. I didn't know what they were chanting. I was thinking how I'd like to hug one of them. So many young women together began to excite me. And for some reason I began thinking about the first time I had sex, in a hotel in Westport when I was a teenager. It had been a fiasco. In the dark, I hadn't been able to read my girlfriend's body with any competence, and after fumbling around for a while, she got so frustrated that she asked me if she should turn on the light and draw me a map.

It's just terrible the thoughts that bedevil a man of forty years when he's suddenly placed in a room with a lot of young women.

Anyway, the prayers came to an end and the people left the room, and I remained, gawping at the garish Buddhas on the walls. I was alone except for a young girl still absorbed in serene contemplation on her cushion. I was examining the wall hangings with my fingers, and gazing at photographs of long-dead monks and poking my nose into the copper bowls of water that stood in a line before the main Buddha on the shrine.

The girl began to move. She put a rainbow-coloured hat on her head, like a tea cosy, and dreadlocks swung either side of her plump cheeks. She was leaving the room. Her lips were purple. I was a spectacle of middle-aged desperation in a brown corduroy jacket. But I didn't care. I had long, unwashed hair. I may have looked like an alcoholic just arrived from the streets of Galway. But the girl was leaving. So I left at the same moment. We were outside putting on our shoes together when I noticed a female Buddha framed in gold just outside the Shrine Room door.

'Who's that?' I asked.

'Tara,' she said.

'I didn't know there was a female Buddha,' I said.

'That's OK,' she said. 'There's a lot you'll have to learn if you've never been involved in Buddhism before.'

'Well, actually,' I said, haughtily, 'I used to be a Catholic priest.'

'That's OK,' she said. As if I had confessed something that required forgiveness.

I learned in time that Jampa Ling had a floating population of beautiful young people with psychological baggage. They were one-winged birds broken by excesses of alcohol or drugs, rudderless from having been dragged up by parents who didn't believe in much or who lived on the edge of disintegration all the time, or just lonely young people who were depressed or disabled in one sense or another. All taking refuge in Buddhist practice and finding great consolation in it. Nothing wrong with that. In fact, a lot of the people there had been genuinely healed, and were strong in mind and body, though I never found out what wounds the girl with the dreadlocks had because I never met her again.

I met lots of other people on my weekly visits for meditation sessions and teachings. Unemployed young people, retired accountants, schoolteachers, women whose husbands had fled with other women, or men who were rebuilding their lives with new partners. I met hippies and Goths and vegetarian couples who lived in cottages around Leitrim making cakes and teaching yoga and learning to be novelists. I drank camomile tea with everyone and learned to sit in the Zen position and, on one occasion, I spent five nights and days in a room on my own upstairs, in silence.

There are times when the drudgery of family life and child-rearing can become oppressive in a small cottage, especially when both partners are working on site. I was in the coal shed writing plays and the beloved was in a galvanised green shed making figures in wax which she would later cast in bronze and present at solo shows around the country. To avoid domestic nuclear meltdown, we sometimes took breaks, from Leitrim and from each other. She would save some money over a few months and then go to the Venice Biennale or some other such international art event while I held the baby. And at other times, I might be invited to give a workshop at some literary festival in Listowel or Donegal.

On this occasion I was on retreat in Jampa Ling, which is where I discovered the beauty and simplicity of water bowls. It was the beginning of autumn. Each morning I woke at 5.30 a.m. and prepared the shrine in the corner of the room – an image of the Buddha, a text of Buddhist teachings, an incense stick, fresh flowers and seven water bowls. I then assumed a meditation posture on my cushion and sat still for half an hour, focusing my attention on my breath. In and out, breathing all the time. In and out. That was it. And the exercise was repeated six times through the day at regular intervals. The bowls were filled, emptied and refilled for each session.

So I sat all day with my water bowls. And I became quite attached to them. Between sessions I studied how not to be attached to anything. And sometimes I dozed on the bed. And every disturbing emotion I experienced in my entire life floated to the surface of my mind at some stage during the five days. Every jealousy, anger and offence in my life rose up during the night and eventually subsided and left me. At the end of the week, I was utterly empty and emotionally cleaned out.

The retreat was also an opportunity to reflect on my life as a writer. After *Sour Grapes*, I wrote one more play for the Abbey Theatre. It was my sixth play at that theatre and it was called *Amazing Grace*, and it was a simple love story between a nurse and a policeman in Fermanagh. I loved working with the Abbey but I also needed to do other things as a writer. Find other ways to tell stories. After all, I was in my mid-forties and I wouldn't have forever.

I was very calm at the end of the retreat and when I went downstairs I was able to focus on every single thing with great ease. I sat in the kitchen gazing at a purple flower in a tiny vase in the centre of the table. It seemed sufficient to make me happy for the rest of my life. And as I walked outside into the garden, and put one foot in front of the other; the colour of the grass, the rustle of the trees and the sound of the birds were all astonishing and wonderful to my ears and eyes. The world was a joy that could not have been more intense if I had been walking on water, and all my preoccupations and worries about being a writer fitted into context. Me and my career were of little significance compared to the astonishing beauty of the world around me.

I thanked the director of the centre, a tall, elderly lady with short grey hair, and confessed that I had found the water bowls very powerful as a tool for prayer. She said that

107

the next time someone was coming from India she would ask them to bring me a special set from the monastery. 'What monastery?' I asked.

She said the spiritual director of the centre had links with a monastery in India, where he went every winter to teach his students there.

'I will phone this evening,' she said, 'and you will have water bowls in a matter of weeks.'

'That won't be necessary,' I replied, 'because in a matter of weeks, I intend to be in India.'

It was a wet November in Leitrim. I stood in the kitchen at home one evening and looked at my beloved and I said, 'There is something very special I want us to do together.'

She had no idea what I was talking about. But I had been thinking about it and planning it for five days and nights.

'We're going to India,' I said, 'for a holiday.'

It was 1997.

I was a regular visitor to Jampa Ling for years, but after I moved to Mullingar, I never returned. For five years, I never paid one visit to the quiet retreat centre in the west Cavan hills. I lost all that. The still mornings and prayer bells and incense. The cat sleeping on a mat in the kitchen as boys with dreadlocks cooked lentils for lunch. Kalash, the dog, scratching himself in the prayer room. Peace and quiet and the warm embrace of broken hearts. Jampa Ling was a place where people could check out from the humdrum of ordinary life and awake in a different way. It was like going fishing. Every time I drove through the gates and up the long tree-lined avenue, I was taking time out. I was letting go. Whereas my adventures in Mullingar were a desperate grasp at life by a middle-aged man in the last-chance saloon. Even before the economic decline, I used to view my bank account online twice a day as I fretted about needing to make more money.

And when the crash came, I had nothing to protect me. I was in Mullingar when Lehman Brothers collapsed, though I didn't know what it meant. And I was in Mullingar when Brian Lenihan and the rest of the government had their notorious midnight meeting about bailing out all the banks in Ireland, though I didn't know what that meant either. All I knew was that since I had come to Mullingar in 2006, the town had been buzzing day and night with trade and entertainment. The shops were always full. The queues at the supermarkets were a nightmare. The taxis never stopped during the weekend and at closing time on Dominick Street, the cars were bumper to bumper. And then came the autumn of 2008.

I went to the doctor one afternoon because I had an ear infection and I mentioned to him that I was feeling rather anxious with all the news on the television. He said it was the stock exchange. He said half the people in his waiting room were there because of the stock exchange. 'They're all worried,' he said. 'Everyone's worried. That makes people ill.'

Numbers were flashing on television screens all day, graphs that nobody could decode. There was a sense that some great tribulation was crossing the face of the earth and would soon strike Mullingar, and sometimes fear of the future tightened the muscles of my heart and gave me a pain in my chest. In the post office, I had an urge to share this with a woman beside me in the queue, but she had her own worries.

'If I hear any more guff on the television about the banks,' she said, 'I'll throw the set out the fucken window.'

I could tell she was a smoker from the smell of her short little breaths. She said, 'Chorus was supposed to come to me on Thursday to change over to the digital and give me a recorder box so that I can watch *EastEnders* in the mornings when the house is quiet. But did they come? No!'

She said, 'If it's not one thing, it's another. My husband was laid off on Friday. He's in the bed this morning and I don't know whether to call him or let him lie there all day. And I got stuck with the grandchild yesterday while me daughter was away at the match. And the child is just getting more attached to me. And I don't want to be landed with that, if you know what I mean. And the boss man has that child ruined – pure spoiled.'

Then her phone rang.

'Oh,' she said, 'so you're up at last.'

I guessed it was boss man.

III

She looked out the window. 'Yeah,' she said, 'I see you. I'll come over to you now.'

She handed me an envelope and fifty cent and said, 'Just put a stamp on that, like a good man.'

After the post office, I cycled towards the bank through a heavy shower and felt consoled that on the surface Mullingar was still unchanged. It still rained on Pearse Street. Someone in the hardware store still put the gas cylinders outside the front door each morning. Old men still walked their little mutts along the canal. People still smoked cigarettes on the streets, and in coffee shops young women from Lithuania still made excellent mochas. Oil lorries still cruised around the housing estates filling up green oil tanks for the winter. And Sky News still carried reports of subprime lenders and the quaking stock markets of the world. When I had come to Mullingar two years earlier, I had bought rabbit ears for the television. Now I was getting high-definition digital images on my thirty-two-inch screen; but the images only wired me to a multitude of anxieties about the global economic situation as the world floated on a sea of delusion.

As I queued in the bank, I strained my neck to absorb breaking news from the flat screen near the ceiling. Apparently Irish bank shares were crashing. Going south. Over twenty years I had put every penny I ever saved into the banks, and I felt helpless now, like someone in steerage listening to dispatches from the bridge of the *Titanic* —

112

Everything is OK, we're just getting the lifeboats ready. Don't you worry.

Outside on Dominick Street, I unlocked my bike and noted the fat purple cloud still hanging in the sky. Either I was about to be drenched again in another terrible downpour, or a spaceship was going to emerge and zap Mullingar to dust. A Romanian man with an accordion positioned himself outside the Ulster Bank and began to play the waltz from the opening of *The Godfather*. I decided to cycle straight home and listen to music on my iPod while I cycled. Then, to ruin an already unpleasant day, my iPod wouldn't work, and that's the thing that annoyed me most. When the bank teller had explained to me that my €20,000 of shares were worth nothing, I had accepted it as if I was the guilty one, like I was a schoolboy who had done something wrong. But I couldn't bear my iPod breaking down.

So when I got home, I phoned a customer support line and was connected to a woman with a warm, gentle voice, and she spoke to me with great kindness.

'Apple have never let me down before,' I said. And she seemed to understand so completely.

I tried to spell Mullingar for her so that she could organise a courier to collect the iPod. Sending a truck to collect an iPod seemed a little extravagant, but I said nothing. Since she didn't seem to know where Mullingar was, I asked her where she was speaking from.

'Bangalore,' she said.

Her gentle voice touched some chord in me. I told her that I had once travelled on the Bangalore Express and had been in the same compartment as Gangubai Hangal, a singer who had sung for Nehru and Gandhi; an old woman dressed in a green sari who wore big glasses like tractor lamps. When she lay down to sleep in the bunk across from mine, she unwound her hair and removed her glasses, and I could see that at eighty, she was still beautiful.

I wanted to ask the woman on the other end of the phone if she sang, but I thought it might be too much of a chat-up line, even at a distance of five thousand miles. But as she went on speaking about the iPod, and the truck and the small print of our contractual agreement, I found her voice so kind and calming that I was overwhelmed with all the things I wanted to tell her. I wanted to tell her that the budget in Ireland had exhausted me, that sorrow comes with age; a kind of sadness I feel every morning. I wanted to tell her that I dreaded old age, and that I saw the fear of death in other people's faces all the time. I wanted to tell her that I felt sad that men run away from their loved ones in late middle age because they are afraid of death, but can't admit it, and then they end up alone in self-centred apartments and die anyway. I wanted to ask her if she'd ever had a curry in the Sherlock Holmes Restaurant in Mumbai. I wanted to tell her that the first time I ever made love was in Mayo, with an American, and I could still remember the day and date distinctly because it was Halloween, the very same day that a helicopter landed in Mountjoy Gaol and flew away with three IRA prisoners in 1973. My American girlfriend of that day had a sticker on her rucksack – Make Love, Not War. We read that as a sign, and drove ourselves into a frenzy of joy between the sheets of a small hotel in Louisburgh later in the evening. Bob Dylan still sings all his songs in my iTunes library, though it's a long time ago since I stood with my torch at the Picnic outside London, singing with him, '… forever young'.

And now I had no iPod and no iTunes and no Bob Dylan. I wanted to tell her that I was all washed up in Mullingar, an outcast from my own youth, and I wanted to tell her that each time I saw snow on the slopes of Leitrim hills, it made me sorrowful because we are all made of dust and the snow will return when we are long gone. And I wanted to tell her that I loved India, and was a great admirer of Buddhist ideas, though my heart still melted for the Mother of Jesus.

115

On Sunday evenings in my early twenties, I used to watch clerical students in Maynooth return from wandering the streets of Dublin, with bric-a-brac and posters they had bought at the Dandelion Market, to warm up their rooms as a substitute for an intimate life. They gathered on winter evenings to chant 'Salve Regina' in a vaulted stone oratory in the seminary. I watched them and was one of them; sorrowful boys that lingered on the edge of a world in which we could never belong. Clutching to the hope of some foggy kindness from heaven that no digital phone could access, because, back then, we did not dream of wireless phones or iPods or casual intimacies with people on the far side of the earth. We dreamed of other things.

I wanted to tell her that when I had been on the Bangalore Express ten years earlier, I was so in love that I thought it would never end. But it did. Because I left my love and fled to Mullingar.

In November 1997 I flew to Mumbai, squashed in with lots of Indians from London who jumped up when the British Airways flight was landing and created such a ruckus trying to get their luggage from the overhead closets and be first off the plane that the air hostesses had to shout at the top of their voices for everyone to sit down in case the movement would affect the landing. I had been able to fund the trip by doing some work on an Indian movie. In exchange for writing some of the script, they gave me an apartment on the north of the city for a few weeks, and enough money to fly my beloved out as well. She arrived when I had the work done about four weeks later.

It was all so astonishing. So miraculous. We were in India. I saw it as a sign. We were being blessed. Some wonderful thing was happening to us. The gods were looking after us.

The truth is that I was still in the grip of magical thinking. Just as I had presumed on the day of my ordination, and just as I had presumed when I first took refuge in the serene quietude of Jampa Ling, that the universe was revolving around me, and the gods were intervening in a multitude of quirky ways to help me along the road of life. So now I also supposed that my beloved and I were conjoined with the blessing of some invisible being. Our lives were being entwined with a grace that almost proved the existence of a benign deity hidden behind the stars.

When I met her at Mumbai Airport, she was distressed because her luggage had gone to Saudi Arabia. I asked about the child. Sophia was then four years old and, rather than bring her to India and expose her to exotic diseases, we left her in the safe company of our neighbours, the Maguire family who lived down the road; a house full of girls where Sophia was embraced like another sister.

'It doesn't matter about the luggage,' I said. 'You can get new clothes. We're in India.'

If there was a god or Buddha, or some divine creature behind the veil of the cosmos, he didn't seem to have much interest in the wretched poor on the streets around us, but it felt like he was holding me in the palm of his hand. I was the one from all the billions on earth that he was keeping his eye on and he was manoeuvring objects in the universe as if they were chess pieces so that the day went well just for little old me. And now my beloved had arrived. Things couldn't be more perfect.

In the back of the taxi, we gushed with amazement at the colours of India. The ocean of human suffering. The miles and miles of shantytown on the route in from the airport and the smell of ten thousand sewers. The sight of people getting out of sleeping bags and canvas tents or crawling out from under sheets of corrugated iron to have their breakfast. Women with toothbrushes stumbling around a tap. Men shitting on the railway tracks.

No matter that the gods chose to ignore the suffering of children with bony stumps instead of hands who stuck their noses to the glass of the taxi at every traffic light. All that mattered was that God had chosen to ignore them all and pay me his full attention. And if there wasn't a God, then my individual reading of Buddhism suggested that the chess pieces in the cosmos were moving themselves magically in orchestrated patterns to my advantage.

The taxi took us to Pali Naka, a curving street on the north of the city with grocery shops all squashed together. We got out and walked from there. The shopkeepers had white coats and the walls and interiors were of dark wood with wall-to-wall drawers, all full of exotic spices. The

119

counters were spread with baskets of dried fruits. Black and wine and purple fruits. Dried raisins. There was a shop selling delicate home-made Punjabi cakes. Outside, the world was a huge bazaar. There were stalls on either side of the street, decked with fruit and vegetables and chickens in cages. There was a telephone shop and a queue of black and yellow taxis. There was a dairy selling fresh yoghurt, and a magazine stand selling second-hand copies of *Time*, *Newsweek* and *India Today*. I saw a statue of the crucified Jesus adorned with saffron paper flowers, which imbued the body of Christ with an erotic energy, a frilly wildlife that reminded me of images that used to surface in mediaeval times in the confessions of canonised nuns who starved their imaginations to sainthood in monastic cells.

'Isn't this just amazing?' I said to my beloved.

Car horns honked aggressively behind us as we walked along the street, sweat pouring down our backs. But we didn't mind. My underpants were soaked in perspiration. But it didn't matter.

I put my arm around the woman with the dark hair and she said she was desperate for a change of clothes, so we found a sari shop and she bought a sari of amber silk, and walked back into the sunlight like a goddess adorned in glory. Such magnificent clothes, we thought, and all for a few rupees.

We reached a leafy avenue, where high walls and gates kept out the rabble, and boys in green security uniforms saluted us as we walked inside with two plastic bags of fruit.

Cozi Home was an elegant set of apartments in two blocks on its own grounds, surrounded by walls and gates and guarded at all times, so that those who lived within could enjoy peace and tranquillity when they returned home in their Japanese jeeps at the end of a long day working in the city.

A young boy in a uniform too big for him washed all the cars and jeeps with a hose every morning. There was an old woman slightly stooped who came to our apartment each day, swept the floors with her twig, washed the dishes, cleaned the toilets and the kitchens and the showers and made more beds than a sailor could make from the sails of a ship.

And the apartment was beautiful. There was a long lounge with sliding glass doors that opened onto a veranda. Below was a sandy tennis court and huge trees for shade and in the near distance the Indian Ocean. The waves were turquoise each evening as the sun, a gigantic ball of crimson, floated like a Chinese lantern just above the horizon. We held hands on the balcony. We made love on the floor. We slept without sheets and ate overripe fruit in the mornings. And after a glorious week, the woman in the amber silk sari and I got on the Bangalore Express. We were getting out of town. We were going on a pilgrimage.

It took us seventeen hours by train to arrive in Hubli Station on our way to the monastery they had told me about in Jampa Ling. Outside the station, there was a small group of beggars, skeletal brown figures in cheap white

121

shirts, slithering around us like fish. We were the only Europeans on the platform, and we decided not to offer any money in case it caused a riot.

Little motorcycles with rear ends like old-fashioned prams lined the pavement down along the sloping street and around the corner.

It was a warm evening. There was an orange glow from the sun. The clutter and the noise of the busy town filled the air. I couldn't hear my own voice above the din of honking cars and children screaming in the dust.

We found a taxi, a big white taxi, and dropped into the huge red leather interior like film stars. It was hot and stuffy and silent. The windows were closed, and like a lord and his lady wife we stared at India through the glass.

The loneliness I had felt in the years we had been together seemed to be dissolving in the heat. All about me, the world groaned in terrible poverty, but behind the glass window of the big white taxi, I had the perverse feeling that the universe was singing with me. And with us.

As dusk settled on the streets and the vendors and promenaders haggled with each other, men stood around shop doors in groups after their day's work and watched the passing white taxi, its horn honking as it negotiated the narrow passages, and the Europeans stared out in wonder.

We arrived in Lama Camp 2 late that night. Monks carried our cases and asked for news from Ireland. How was their teacher? Was he in good health? They had been expecting us because he had telephoned earlier to say we would be arriving that night. We were their honoured guests because we had come from Ireland, as ambassadors of their teacher.

We were brought to a square two-storey building with single rooms which housed 108 monks. There was a Prayer Room on the upper floor and one toilet on the ground floor. The cement walls were not painted. Mattresses lined the floors and three monks were squashed into each room.

In the entire campus, which constituted three separate monasteries, there was a population of almost 3,000 monks, and in the evenings hundreds of them strolled along the dusty roads that stretched through vast flat meadows between the individual monasteries. They talked of dairy cows and milk. They showed us fields of lush grass and explained that they had brought the grass on trains from other parts of India. They wanted rich fields to feed cattle, and they tried numerous times to reseed the land, but it hadn't worked. So they literally re-covered acres with turf that they had brought across India by train.

They apologised for the toilets, which were in a rough condition. They said they were hoping to build a new hostel soon, with western-standard toilets.

Many of the young monks had TB and seemed gaunt and weak. Others were stout and robust and surrounded us from the time we woke until we went to bed at night.

In the Prayer Room each morning, I sat with them as they chanted their prayers. I was overwhelmed. I cried. I

123

hugged my beloved. Everything was wonderful. The blaze of sunshine, the prayer halls, libraries, the prayer flags flapping on every building.

One particular young monk kept close to us at all times. He had smooth, hairless skin, an oval face and eyes like brown berries dipped in a pool of almond milk. The woman in the amber sari loved watching him and he gazed at her with a concentration that was neither hostile nor sentimental. He spoke no English but had a way of gesturing, a theatricality, which enabled him to communicate easily. He laughed when she didn't understand him. And he laughed when she did understand him. He was always laughing. Especially when he was talking about religious life. But when he spoke about cooking, his body swelled with visceral intensity and his tongue became like a warrior's sword.

They even cooked us a banquet one evening. After spending all afternoon in the heat outside the hostel, chopping meat and vegetables on wooden boards, they fried it all up and set it out on ornate dishes at a long table, and placed me and my beloved at the centre, and they sat around and they hugged us in one enormous collective hug.

And afterwards we went up to the Prayer Room and offered prayers to Tara, the female Buddha, framed in glass and lit by a hundred butter candles. It was the same image as I had first seen in Jampa Ling when I met the girl with the plump cheeks and the tea cosy hat. I offered auspicious white scarves, with almost one hundred monks standing

124

around me, boys and old men with grey hair, in maroon robes mumbling their prayers. I watched the monks and my wife watched me. And then she and I shared a gaze, an open, joyful gaze of astonishment. We were witnessing something extraordinary but what mattered was that we were witnessing it together. We were sharing a moment. All the monks in all the world were suddenly of less importance than her. All the Buddhas in all the universe were of less relevance than her. I was not alone in this exotic world. I was sharing it with someone else. *Maybe this is why people go on holidays together*, I thought.

The winter sun was like an orange, low in the sky, and the haycocks threw long shadows on the shaven yellow grass, and I walked with my love on the dusty roads between one prayer hall and another.

In an empty space one morning, we saw an old monk sitting on his cushion with a copy of the Prajnaparamita scripture. Beside him was a young schoolgirl in a western-style grey school uniform. Both of them were reciting. The monk whispered in Tibetan and the girl whispered words in English. She was learning her grammar. The two languages blended. The old man and the young girl were like a choir in harmony. My own daughter came to mind and, for a moment, I missed her. I imagined her sitting on a neighbour's lap, enjoying her pasta back in Ireland. Tears welled up in my eyes and the old man noticed me and was distracted from his prayer, so I fled the building.

Just outside the Prayer Room, in the porch there was a long, dripping hive of bees. The hairless young monk told me later that the Dalai Lama had stood in the same spot just a few weeks earlier and asked about the bees. *How long had the bees been there? Were they dangerous?*

'Yes,' the hairless monk had said, 'they were dangerous.'

So they asked the Dalai Lama if the bees should be displaced.

'No,' he had said. 'Leave them where they are.'

We all looked up at the dangerous bees. I looked. And the hairless monk looked. And the woman in the sari looked. Stinging bees. I needed nothing else in life at that moment. Except perhaps water bowls.

That night there was a knock on the door. I opened it and found an old monk in the darkness outside. In his two cupped hands, he held something wrapped in a white silk scarf. His grey hair was shaved to the roots. His eyes were narrow and his mouth quivered, and he was toothless. Flecks of masticated food stained the front of his maroon robe. I recognised him as the monk who had been with the young girl.

'I saw you today,' he said.

'Yes,' I admitted. 'That was me.'

'Yes. You.'

'Me.'

'You.'

'Yes.'

We laughed. His eyes scanned the room behind me and the sleeping body of my wife in one of the twin beds.

'Long time in prison,' he said, pointing to himself.

'How long?'

He didn't understand my question.

'Were you ten years in prison?' I wondered.

'Yes.'

'Were you twenty years in prison?'

'Yes.'

I tried again.

'How long were you in prison?'

'Always in prison,' he said, and broke into a great laugh that almost woke the woman in the bed.

'Please,' he said, 'take this.'

He stretched out his hands and I opened the silk scarf and saw seven water bowls.

'Thank you.'

'What's up?' the wife asked, in her sleep.

I wanted to say more but the old monk put his finger to his lips.

'The mosquitoes are coming in,' the wife said.

'Sleep,' the old man said, and then he closed the door. I did not hear his footsteps as he went down the stairs or around the side of the building under our window or back along the gravel path towards his building. *He must be a light sleeper*, I thought, *and a swift traveller in the dark*.

After that we left the monastery. *It was a kind of poetry,*

127

I thought. There was no more to be done or seen and we were scheduled to leave the following day. The pilgrimage was complete. And perfect.

The young hairless monk left us to the train. We had time to kill, so we went to a cheap café and ate rice and dhal and drank tea in small glasses that a seven-year-old boy served us at the table. The boy, with an abundance of shining brown hair, carried twenty-four glasses of tea in his wire rack as he moved from one table to another in his bare feet.

The young monk stood on the platform until the train moved off. I stood at the carriage door, clutching the white silk scarf he had placed around my neck at his last farewell, and I waved as the train began to move. The water bowls were in the bottom of the suitcase.

Gangubai Hangal was on the train travelling with her daughter. She was one of India's most famous classical singers. As she was getting onto the train, a man in a suit threw himself at her feet and kissed her toes and then stood up and offered her flowers. She took them graciously and came on board and entered our compartment. We were travelling together. It was just another sign. She told us she was going to Mumbai to partake in a great felicitation for some other famous singer. She ate oranges and perched on the top bunk and dangled her feet like a schoolgirl. That night she robed in a long cream nightdress and let her grey hair down on her shoulders. I woke once and saw her across from me, staring at me.

In the morning the train stopped outside Mumbai, and vendors lined the platform with all kinds of breakfast. Omelettes, sausages, fried bread and tea, or rice dishes and a variety of fruit. They were small, thin men with white shirts and bare feet or flip-flop sandals, and some with fiercely manicured moustaches. They flitted through the carriages shouting their wares, and Gangubai and her daughter bought more oranges. I went onto the platform and ordered an omelette from a man who was frying the eggs on a pan which was attached to the rear of his tricycle, but I almost missed the train as it pulled out. I ran with the bread and omelette in one hand and jumped in the open door, and flopped down beside my lady in the amber sari. And I laughed so loud that Gangubai Hangal looked slightly uneasy at me. But I was happy. Happier than I had ever been in my life.

We went to Juhu Beach that evening by rickshaw, me and my beloved, through fishing villages of two-storey houses with low roofs jutting out over open rooms and balconies where caged birds sang and small icons of the Virgin Mary with white plastic flowers adorned the gable walls. There were rows of small iron huts and baskets of fish on the side of the road. The fish were being gutted by women who crouched at stone benches and cats beneath the benches devoured the guts. There were rows of huts where car mechanics worked all day on Mercedes, Toyotas and old Russian jeeps. Each vehicle was deconstructed into nuts and bolts and rods and rims. The ground was covered with the innards of engines. Backsides were stuck up in the wind and heads vanished under bonnets. Young boys smoked and watched the skilled workers, and learned by holding things. We held hands in the back of the rickshaw, as fiercely as we had thirteen years earlier when we'd first met in Annaghmakerrig. The world was in love as we were in love.

On the beach, there were Islamic women in black cloaks prostrating in the direction of Mecca. There were monkeys on chains. Elephants on ropes. Stalls selling Coca-Cola and loudspeakers pumping out Madonna and The Cranberries. There were bananas stacked on a small man's shoulders as he struggled under the weight, and a boy was selling bamboo flutes. There were horses with bells and buggies with bunting, all yellow and white flapping in the wind. The buggies had bicycle wheels and the horses galloped the length of the beach as romantic couples screamed and held their hats. We were in love. The world was in love. And full of beautiful people. Thousands of people. Ordinary people in simple shirts and trousers, sandals and saris, holding hands, scolding children, licking ice-creams and strolling around without worry or direction.

That was the eve of our return to Ireland. And that night India won a cricket match against South Africa in Mumbai and the sky exploded with fireworks and young men shouted and roared and danced in the streets. The world rejoiced as we rejoiced, and we rejoiced with all around us. All the way back to the apartment in the rickshaw, little bombs exploded on either side of us. Sulphur in the air. Clouds of blue and red smoke. The rickshaw racing through it all like a chariot. We watched Mumbai from the veranda, crackling and sparkling and singing at the top of its voice. A long scream. The roar of traffic like a rejoicing animal's roar. A lion in the mountains. And a plume of smoke over it all.

'What are you thinking?' she asked me.

I couldn't say. For me, the world had become a beautiful place. I walked in it safely now. I walked in it deeply, because I wasn't alone. Back in Ireland, my adventures in coal sheds, Catholic churches or Buddhist retreat centres had all been solitary acts – but here in India, what really mattered was us. I was holding her hand. We were like young lovers again who cared nothing about clergy or police or growing old; lovers who lived their dream in every waking moment. Who become self-less in sexual ecstasy, and who lost their individual existence in the gaze of the other. And as we boarded the plane in Mumbai bound for London, I had seven beautiful water bowls in my luggage that I would line up along the shelf in my room and fill to the brim every morning when I got home with pure, clear water.

That was the plan.

But the water bowls never worked. That illusion crumbled when I landed back in Leitrim on a wet Thursday afternoon in December and resumed ordinary life. In fact, the intensity of joy I had experienced in India only accelerated a further descent into the dark. There is a way in which holiday time can leave two lovers deeply exposed, because in heightened worlds all boundaries dissolve. And then when ordinary mundane life is resumed, there is an opposite reaction: a rush for cover, a wish to protect one's privacy again.

Why do men hide from their lovers? Why do they fear

to show emotion? Why do they run with terror from the body of a woman? Why do they need God to sustain them in that isolation? I don't know. But I know this is what I did. I did all those things for years before I went to India. And in India I moved out from my own self and became absorbed in the presence of another being; it was an ecstasy outside time. But when the ecstasy was over, the dishes had to be washed. And after the saffron and turquoise of India, the skies over Leitrim never seemed so completely grey.

I put away the water bowls on a remote shelf in my office, where they oxidised over the years and lost their shine. We kept some of the wall hangings and the Buddha statues we had taken home, and placed them around the house above bookshelves or over the television, but they were artefacts of another culture now, almost ironic in an artistic sort of way.

To earn some money, I became writer-in-residence with Roscommon County Council. Each morning, I headed out to some far-away town where there was a library. Sometimes I might lunch on chips and beans in various cafés around the county. Places full of pimpled lanky boys and tidy pig-tailed girls in grey school uniforms. Afterwards I would spend the afternoons meeting creative writing groups in the hush of damp libraries with green walls. Dead-end libraries as comfortable as old sheds. Musty-smelling bookshelves. Old women browsing through romantic novels. The librarian whispering on the telephone behind her desk. And old men turning the pages of gardening books.

The road home in the evening was dotted with large, modern houses. The middle classes loved their glass extensions and wood-panelled interiors. Rugs and florid sofas were lit up for all to see. It was the turn of the century. Everyone seemed to be doing well. At least I envied everyone.

One night in September, I stopped in Ballintubber. I parked beside a white wall. There was a grimy-green glass window in the wall. A delph statue of the Queen of Peace wearing white robes and a golden crown smiled out at me. I went up to Garvey's pub for a drink. A cosy bar with fogged glass and old-style timber beams and glowing whiskey bottles behind the bar, where men sat in semi-darkness staring into their pints.

I drank a single pint in silence amid the plumes of blue smoke that hung in the air. A few farmers on high stools beside me remained equally morose. Not even drink could stir their old faces into life. Eventually, I drove home and threw myself into bed.

She was awake and uneasy in the bed beside me. Her eyes were open but they didn't say much. I lay awake staring at the ceiling. She did the same. The amber silk sari was hanging in the wardrobe in mothballs.

The following day, I opened the door of another library and met Mrs Eglington, who was looking for a detective book and whispering as if she were in church. And a retired teacher was standing behind a bookcase in the local history section. Mrs Eglington was an elderly lady with blue hair and a green tweed overcoat up to her neck, and she was now talking to the librarian about the death penalty.

'All criminals should be executed,' she said. 'Not just Karla Tucker, whoever she is. And young people from poor backgrounds who are not able for secondary school, because they don't have the brains, should be given a working trade and strict discipline,' she added. 'Learning only confuses some people,' she said to me as I approached.

'You're dead right there, Mrs Eglington,' I said. And then I gathered them all in a circle to begin the class. Mrs Eglington led the conversation, firstly addressing the issue of the death penalty and latterly the availability of cream buns.

'Can't get a cream bun in Roscommon nowadays,' she said. 'In Dublin, there was no end of cream buns. When I was in the Department of Education, I could just run across the street for a cream bun. Imagine that. Right in the middle of the city. And here we are with cows on every side of us and not a cream bun to be had.'

Driving home through Castlerea that night, I turned on the radio.

'There's something going on in Texas tonight,' the disc jockey said.

'Oh good,' I said. I was glad there was something happening somewhere.

'An execution!' he said.

'Well, holy shit,' I whispered as I drove through the blanket of drizzle and the puddles and potholes.

'Thousands of miles away in Texas, Karla Tucker will be executed in six hours and forty minutes' time.'

'No kidding.'

'She lived in a mobile home. Killed her husband there over a decade ago.'

I wondered what he would say next.

'I've a great admiration for Texas music,' he said, and then he played a record called 'Hank Williams Said It Best'.

My wife was still sitting by the fire when I got home. I made a sandwich in the kitchen and joined her.

'Any news?' she asked.

'Yes,' I said. 'They're going to kill Karla Tucker. Four forty-five Irish time. If you're interested.'

I went to bed. Slept all night. Got up at eight and turned on the radio. There was no news from Texas. Karla Tucker had dropped off the headlines. Karla Tucker was no more and Texas was a different country.

My wife was still in bed and the child was whingeing. The dishwasher was so full that I couldn't get my cornflakes bowl into it, and so I washed it in the sink. Outside the leaves had not yet begun to fall, and everything in the garden was still and ready for the rain that was coming. There was no avoiding the world in all its ugliness. It embraced Karla Tucker and me and everyone else with savage indifference.

It was September 2010. I was fifty-seven. I had been in Mullingar for four years. It was my fourth year as a columnist with *The Irish Times*. I was workshopping a new one-man show. My daughter was beginning her Leaving Certificate year. She had become deeply involved in equestrian life. If her dream had been to jump in horse shows, then she had fulfilled it many times over, because every weekend she was up and down the country jumping in various SJI shows, taking lessons with Ian Fearon, and eventually winning a place on an Irish junior squad that would be jumping in an international competition in Paris in the spring of 2011. After two years in the apartment I had found a large old nineteenth century house a few miles outside the town which was so big that sometimes I forgot I was sharing it with my daughter. There were so many old rooms and corridors and stairways that it felt as if I was living alone. And we were close to the stable yards where the daughter spent most of her time. Her mother came at the weekends and for the first time in our lives we had no worries about money. And then everything went wrong.

The battle took place in my body. The first thing I noticed was impotence. That's something that draws a man's attention fairly quickly. One night I had feelings and sensations like a normal man, the next night I was limp. And nothing I did or imagined had any effect.

I made a pot of tea, and tried to excuse myself by saying I was tired. In the morning I got on with the day as normal. I guessed my prostate might be causing difficulties. It had been irritating me for years. I would go to the toilet three times a night. If I took a few pints of beer in the pub, I wouldn't be able to endure the taxi home without having to stop at least once.

So I guessed the impotence was due to that. I took Viagra. That worked a few times but it was a numbing experience, which is not exactly what sex is supposed to be. I functioned. But, to be truthful, I didn't find much fun in it.

And then I went to Shanghai. That was a mistake. I had

138

enough work to be going on with in theatre, but when I was offered a week in China, just to play a flute in a theatre show, I couldn't resist. After one of the performances, I went for a meal with the woman who had been working with us as a translator. We chose a fish restaurant and the carcass that arrived on a plate with almond sauce looked like something dragged up from the wreck of the *Titanic*. We talked of things forbidden in China, and of delicious foods and the excesses of emperors and I returned to my hotel in splendid form. But an hour later, I was stuck to the toilet, and the toilet was destroyed.

My flight was early the next day, and it was a miracle that I found someone who could get me strong tablets that held things together until I got home. I explained to the taxi man that things were fragile. And I explained to the air hostesses that things were fragile.

The next bad sign was the weekend. I went to a swanky hotel with the wife for a break. Sophia was staying with friends who kept horses near Mullingar, something she did often. They would spend the weekend exercising the animals, cleaning stables and watching *X Factor* in the evening while eating pizzas.

The wife and I had a four-poster bed. The spa had a communal jacuzzi, a cool pool, a seaweed pool, two saunas and what the brochure described as a 'heavenly hot tub'. She went to everything. I lay on the four-poster and groaned until she returned.

'You're not well,' she said.

'It's just the flu,' I said.

But it wasn't the flu.

That Christmas, I was still in decline. I had no energy. Snow covered the big old stone house and the laurel hedges and the old chestnut trees, and the fields all around us were hidden by massive white blankets and, though I usually respond to snow with the delight of a child, on this occasion it just made me miserable. The water pipes were frozen. We had to drive to a stable yard to fill containers of water from a tap used for the horses. And when the usual guests and family members arrived, I found the cooking a chore I could barely tolerate, never mind having to be nice to everyone for three entire days. I drank a lot of wine to keep up the spirits but even that didn't work very well. When the guests were leaving, I barely bothered wishing them a Happy New Year. I was just glad to see them all go.

At the end of January, I was performing in *The Tinker's Curse*, a one-man show in Garter Lane, Waterford. It was the beginning of a long tour. A week later, I was in the Watergate Theatre in Kilkenny. I booked into a cheap guesthouse and went to the theatre as usual and did my warm-ups on stage and then sat in the dressing room waiting for the audience to come in. Finbar Coady, the musician who accompanied me in the show, watched me uneasily. He asked if I was all right. I said I was a bit tired.

I felt a tickle in my throat, and an irritation in my chest.

140

It stayed with me through the performance. I could hear my voice running short of breath. When we were finished, I went for a drink and after my third trip to the toilet, Finbar asked again if I was OK. I said I might have a cold coming on.

'Go back to the guesthouse and have a good rest,' he said. So I did. I went to the guesthouse and drank a Lemsip in bed before falling asleep. The next day was cold and wet. I stayed under the covers but couldn't keep warm. Eventually I went to the landlady for extra blankets and a heater. I went to the theatre at 4 p.m. as usual. I just about got through the show, but things were getting worse. I was tired and miserable. Finbar said he was worried. I said, 'I'll take a day in bed and I'll be fine.'

A week later, I was at home in Mullingar but still in bed. And I could hardly breathe. I went to the doctor and he gave me antibiotics, a course for five days. In the meantime, I had another show in Dún Laoghaire. I took the tablets and drove up the M50 and did the show. It went well and I was in great form afterwards.

In fact, I was so elated the following evening that I decided to go out to a party. I asked someone if drink would affect the antibiotics. Not if you don't take them at the same time as the drink, they told me. An answer which suited me fine.

Two days later, I went for a walk into town along the Royal Canal. I wanted to push my body a bit now that I

141

had recovered. I wanted to get back into shape because we had more theatre shows coming up on our tour. I had a coffee in the Greville Arms and walked home.

It was a round trip of about two hours. At the end of it, my body was stiff. I sat on the sofa and experienced a strange sensation, like a fog seeping into my back. It felt as if my spine was leaking gas into my chest and lungs and belly and then into every muscle in my arms and legs. I felt heavy. Stiff. I can't describe it any better than by saying it was like a fog spreading all through my limbs. I could barely get up the stairs and into bed.

The next day, I had an interview with an old lady in Kinnegad. I was doing a video project at the time with elderly people, recording their stories with a view to making an archive of folklore for the libraries.

I arrived in Kinnegad at 11 a.m. The lady was ready for me, all dressed up and her hair done, as she sat with the chairwoman of the local Active Age Committee in Serenity House. I took the camera from the jeep and set it up in the day room and sat behind it and asked some questions and the old lady talked enthusiastically to camera about her life as a young person long ago. But I could barely follow what she was saying. I was drifting in and out of consciousness, without realising it.

At lunchtime I called to the greengrocer. He said, 'You look grey. You have aged ten years since Christmas.'

'I just need antibiotics.'

So I went to the doctor and he gave me more. I went home to bed and took the tablets and lay there for another week. But each day I was just as exhausted as the day before. There was no improvement. The tablets didn't seem to be working. I phoned the doctor and told him I had a performance scheduled for the following Wednesday. I needed something stronger than antibiotics. He gave me steroids. Little red tables with instructions to take two the night before the show, two on the morning of the show and two just after the show. And it was a great show. I don't know what the audience thought, but I was completely out of my head and we got a standing ovation.

A week later I had a gig in Hearn's Hotel in Clonmel. A week later in the Excel in Tipperary. And then on to Kilmallock. And on and on and on. The show, as they say, must go on.

By May, my back was giving me trouble. It began in Mullingar in a Spanish restaurant at lunch. I felt a sudden pain in the side as if I had pulled a muscle. Later in the afternoon, I realised my back was swollen. I put mysterious ointment on it, which I had got from a Chinese friend. The muscle heated up wonderfully and I thought I'd be fine in the morning. But the following morning I couldn't move. I couldn't get out of bed. It felt as if discs in my spine were out of place. It felt as if my arm was out of its socket. It felt as if muscles all over were torn or damaged.

I went to an osteopath. And I went to a chiropractor.

143

The chiropractor crunched my torso this way and that way to establish if it was damaged. It wasn't. According to him, I was fine. I had simply put my body under too much pressure from bad posture, and I needed to fix that. He recommended a girdle which could be bought in a particular pharmacy; a strong elastic pad that wrapped around the body at the waist.

'Wear it two hours a day and take a few paracetamol tablets to reduce the swelling.' I asked him if it would be OK to take a few painkillers as well when I was doing a show.

'Oh yes,' he said. 'No bother.' He told me that he treated a referee from time to time who always needed a few ibuprofen to get him through football matches.

This was handy because I had a stash of ibuprofen, which a friend had got from a chemist, unofficially, under the counter to save me money.

I went on doing the show at the Mermaid Arts Centre in Bray and Howth Golf Club and for three nights at the Civic in Tallaght and, finally, in Ballymun. It was coming to the end of May. Since February I had spent my life in bed or travelling to various gigs or standing on stage performing the show.

The nineteenth-century farmhouse I lived in was a big empty space and the walls are made of solid stone. The mantelpiece in the front drawing room is shoulder high. It required enormous buckets of coal to keep the place warm. There were two sofas. The curtains were hung on brass rings and looked ragged and dowdy. For that reason, I rarely went downstairs. I remained either in the bed or the bathroom.

The prostate was blocking the normal process of passing water and made each night a dreadful experience. I got up almost every hour to urinate in pain and return to bed, knowing I had not voided my bladder and would be up again in another hour.

And there was no en suite. The bathroom was a long walk away; down one set of stairs and up another. I treaded that path four or five times each night in the dark. I thought it was normal. I thought it was part of ageing. Part of having an infection. Eventually I left a bucket in the corner of the room.

Sometimes in the afternoons, I got up for a few hours and went downstairs to the television in the front room. I watched Anna Netrebko in *La Traviata* over and over again and I cried much more than was normal even for me. My chest was constantly congested. My eyes were watering. My head was hot. My limbs were sore. And there was always another performance just five or six days away.

There was no question of throwing in the towel. I strapped on my girdle and swallowed my ibuprofen, and the antibiotics, but I never joined up the dots. The GP didn't join up the dots. He spent most of our consultation time staring at a computer screen and he always delivered antibiotics if I needed them.

145

In early May, I was in Ballymun Axis theatre for three nights. After the third night, I drove home with enormous red rashes on my left leg above my knee. I went to the doctor again the following day.

'It's either shingles or cellulitis,' he declared.

So he gave me a course of antibiotics for shingles, and another course for cellulitis. And a few painkillers as well. Off I went to the chemist and got the prescription, which now amounted to thirteen tablets a day. I set the alarm on my iPhone and swallowed a different tablet every hour. I was regressing to some childhood state of acceptance, whereby I was doing something that was wrong but I had not the strength to assert myself and say, 'Stop, you're hurting me.'

Nobody was hurting me. I was hurting myself.

Apart from performing in *The Tinker's Curse*, I spent most of 2011 between late January and the end of May in bed in a large room, with deep-red velvet curtains keeping out the sunshine, a pisspot in the corner of the room, and a lot of medicines, tablets, ointments and boxes of tissues. Food came on a tray, served by my wife whose identity dissolved over time. She became abstract. A person without title or function. I lost any previous relationship I'd had with her and became a dependant. She was the woman who came with the tray, who changed the sheets, who cleaned the pyjamas, who went to the chemist, and who made the smoothies and the soups.

At night I had bad dreams and I recorded them all. I listened to Radio 3 a lot, and sometimes surfed YouTube for lectures on psychology or Buddhism. I spent hours just daydreaming and trying to hold my identity together.

It was unclear to me why I kept thinking of my father, but I did. It's as if I had unfinished business with him. As if my memories were shrouded in fog and I could not quite see him clearly. Sometimes at night, I dreamed he was in the room. Sometimes I would be returning from the bathroom with only the light of my iPhone to light the corridor and I would sense my father's ghost, lurking in the shadowy well of the stairs.

My father was reared by a severe grandmother who would barge into any neighbour's house and lift the lids off their pots to see what they were cooking. He didn't marry until he was almost fifty, so by the time I came along, he may have thought about me as an idea rather than as something to hold or cuddle, and so I grew up, more or less, in what sociologists call a 'non-touching family', where if you happened to brush your foot against another person's leg below the dinner table, you immediately apologised. As a child my personal space was more secure than a military bunker, which is very likely why I went into my teenage years without the remotest understanding of love.

No matter how many times I heard it in lyrics of The

Beatles, the word 'love' never made me sweat, swoon or palpitate as a teenager; it just made me nervous. Love was some kind of invisible object to be contemplated but never touched, like the wafer on the golden plate every Sunday morning. Love was theological, ontological and almost as precious as the Waterford Crystal in the china cabinet that my mother forbade anyone to touch; fluted glasses given to her on her wedding day, the sacraments of a remembered love. She protected them from dust and breakage by placing them under lock and key and I often sat on the floor as a child gazing in at them in the cabinet, though it would have been out of the question to hope that I could ever touch them, never mind play with them.

My mother, much later in life, looked into that same cabinet one day and imagined that the glasses had changed shape. And since that could not be, she then deduced that someone had robbed the originals and replaced them with inferior work. One way or another, she never looked at that china cabinet again without feeling profoundly unhappy.

As soon as I could, I fled from that suburbia of restrained emotion and found refuge in the mountains of west Cavan, where, instead of posturing around china cabinets in a drawing room, people huddled around Stanley ranges in kitchens, where men with blue fingers ate big lumps of bacon between slices of thick bread, and lambs in cardboard boxes sucked milk from bottles, and pet donkeys nuzzled the window looking for oranges, and there was always a

149

black and white border collie under one of the chairs, who eyed me cautiously, because I wasn't like the others; I didn't rub behind his ears or scratch his belly or tease him with bones from my plate.

I never liked dogs. But if Sam, the black Labrador, had not farted the night I was reading the life story of the Dalai Lama, I would not have retired to the bedroom, the daughter would not have followed me, we would never have had a conversation about horses and I would never have ended up in Mullingar.

I cringed with horror the first time my daughter, at the age of five, pleaded with me to get a dog.

I said, 'No!'

And then she insisted, and I said, 'Definitely not!'

And she looked me in the eye and said, 'Ah, Dad, go on.'

And I said, 'What kind do you want?'

So I was forced to live with a black Labrador for five years in order to maintain domestic harmony and satisfy my child's need for company after school. But what really troubled me was the way a big dog with short hair could manage to expose his private parts, as he stretched himself at the fire, and the level of noise he could make when he chose to groom his nether regions during the *Late Late Show*. There were times when it was hard to hear the scintillating cut and thrust of conversation on the television, because of the din yer man made in the corner, sucking everything clean.

And thus my mind wandered and rambled round in circles

as I lay in bed, and the weeks went by. A car would come at 4 p.m. to drive me to Dublin, whenever I had a performance.

'Don't talk to me on the way up,' I would say. 'I want to conserve my energy.'

There was a rocking chair on stage so that if my back pain got too severe, I could sit down in the middle of the show. Afterwards someone drove me home and I felt ecstatic. I felt I had achieved something enormous, because I had fulfilled the engagement. And stayed on my feet.

Which was an illusion. Because I wasn't on my feet at all. I was in bed for months. And always I returned to the bed. The seasons were changing and I was still lying there. The BBC became my great consolation, because I love their accents, their vowels and their soft voices. I love waking up in a world where music matters rather than politics.

Although even politics was interesting on the BBC. They had a more global perspective than Irish radio. Listening to Arundhati Roy speak on the plight of poor people in India moved me to tears, and made me feel ashamed of my own trivial suffering. But I tired of the radio too and I would just lie in the bed, gazing out the window at the green bushes that lined the canal and the far hills and hardwood trees along the sloping ditches.

One Saturday afternoon in April, there wasn't a breath of wind, not even the slightest movement in the trees. From my bed, I could see that the walkway along the canal was deserted. There were no old men walking dogs or ladies panting in tracksuits. I saw just one man in the distance. So far away that I could not make out any details. He had fishing tackle with him and a fold-up chair. He sat on his chair and cast his rod. If he'd looked up, he would have seen a big house in the distance. He would not have known that I was behind the window, watching him. After a while, he stood up and walked about twenty metres to a tree. Beneath this tree, he took out a cigarette and smoked. He looked up at the sky a lot. When he was finished, he returned to his seat. He did the same thing every forty minutes. Always smoking at the same tree. Always looking at the sky. I don't know what he was thinking of. He didn't know I was watching him. And yet it was a comfort to me that he was there.

I remember heading for a gig in Kilmallock in May. I was in a fog of antibiotics and painkillers. It was as if a glass wall was coming down between me and the rest of the world, but I drove all the way there myself.

That night I booked in to an old hotel. Somewhere I could be both close to other people and yet utterly alone. In the middle of the night, I heard people orgasming in distant rooms, just as a dying person might hear children playing outside the window. I felt that at last I had become a ghost. Just like my father. And soon I might join him in the shadows. Or else he would appear to me. Though neither option seemed at all attractive.

On 1 June, I was in Dublin for lunch with an actor

friend. I was having a bowl of green pea soup, and either the actor or the soup reminded me of a poem by Lewis Carroll, in *Through the Looking-Glass*.

> 'The time has come,' the Walrus said,
> 'To talk of many things:
> Of shoes – and ships – and sealing-wax
> Of cabbages – and kings –
> And why the sea is boiling hot –
> And whether pigs have wings.'

I didn't say this to the actor. He might have thought I was losing my mind. Instead I just said, 'I don't think I'm well today.' And I excused myself and got an early train home, where after a grotesque attempt at eating a quiche, I went to the toilet and began bleeding from my back passage. I was taken to A&E where I lay on a trolley for the night, amid the usual bedlam of groaning humanity, blood in the toilets and heroic nurses. 153

They gave me painkillers and tied me to a drip, and in a short while I floated through the looking glass. Around my trolley, I saw my father's ghost again and many Christian saints in pain and agony and a battalion of dainty teapots endlessly moving up and down the corridor.

'How's them guts?' a doctor in a blue hat asked me.

'Doctor,' I said, 'it's running out of me like crude oil.'

1 June 2011, it was almost midnight. I was bleeding from the back passage. I was lying on a trolley. I said to the beloved, 'You go home and have a rest. There's no point in you being here.'

Earlier a doctor had said, 'This could be catastrophic.'

I was frightened. We were both frightened. But she went away, and the nurses put cot sides on my trolley and wheeled me and my drip into the corner of a linen room, where it wasn't as busy, and where I tried to sleep. But I couldn't. The nurses came and went, and chatted about their children and their days off and on, and gossiped about various doctors. I kept my eyes closed and listened, and for some reason I was almost happy there, in the cot, amid the smell of freshly laundered sheets and towels with strange women watching over me.

One of the most common questions women ask is: *What are you thinking?*

One of the most common answers men give is: *Nothing.*

Men go on fishing trips and hunting expeditions, trying to find the warrior or wild man whom they avoided in youth. Trying to chase the ghost of the man they might have been. But it never works. All they do is catch fish or kill deer, and bring the dead home like trophies to some woman who doesn't quite appreciate the romance behind a dead carcass lying on her kitchen table, any more than she might appreciate the cat coming in and dropping dead mice at the bedroom door.

I never did fishing or hunting, but I turned away from the beloved a thousand times. 'What are you thinking?' she would say, trying to decipher what might be going on behind my brooding eyes. And I would lie.

'Nothing, dearest. Nothing at all.'

I went to Chicago one time on my own, about five years after we were married. I flew into O'Hare Airport on a cold afternoon in early January and phoned Norshore Cabs from the lobby of the airport. I had no cents and had to ask

155

a fat policeman how to use the phone. It was windy and dry and the taxi man was from Mumbai. He said the snow was coming.

The apartment was near the lake. It belonged to a friend and she had posted me the key and details about how to open doors. Locks. Neighbours. Landings. Lights. The fridge. And not to lift the kettle off the ring without a tea towel. And Tasha's phone number. A note beside the phone said: 'Make yourself at home. Call Tasha in the morning and she will look after you.'

I showered the following morning and phoned. Tasha was Russian. She said we should meet at one o'clock. In the restaurant, a Mexican waitress was putting away the Christmas decorations, going along the wire to each bulb and placing it in the allotted socket in the cardboard box. Untangling the wires. Tasha was forty and overweight, but she sat like a little girl, bundled up in her woollies, with two enormous brown eyes in a face of delicious smooth, sallow skin. Her facial expressions were almost hidden beneath the chaotic fringe of uncombed black hair streaked with grey. She stood up and we greeted each other like old comrades. She was beautiful and anarchic and compassionate all in one big embrace. Then we sat at the Formica table. Her eyes drooped. I pretended to read the menu. I counted three layers of cardigan. Like she was just out of bed. We had omelettes. She was shy until it came to ordering rashers.

'I cannot get into their minds here in America,' she said, 'that I do not like burned bacon.'

'Raw,' she said. 'Give it to me raw!'

Something was drawing us together. We ate in silence. Finally she spoke.

'Do you believe in God?'

'No,' I said.

'Well,' she said, 'we must try.'

We both laughed. The moment of love came on the sidewalk. When we both stood staring at the snowflakes.

'I suffer depression,' she said.

'So do I,' I heard myself muttering. Vodka came to mind. The two of us in a dark cosy bar, all afternoon. A Russian woman trying to believe in God, and an Irishman trying not to believe in God. I was so close to her lips, her hair, her smell and her big brown eyes.

'No,' she said. 'I have a music lesson. I teach violin.'

A long protracted moment in which I might have said, *Ah, go on. Let's risk it.*

And a lifetime would have fallen apart. Because you can fall in love on a holiday, when you're out of context and in a strange land. And you meet someone whose path in life has been identical. And you don't have to say what you're thinking because they know what you're thinking. And you know her more intimately than your own soul. But I let her go. You must let her go. And I watched her walk down the slippery sidewalk as the wind blew dusty snow around

157

her in a great angry swirl, which could have been the hand of the invisible God she was still trying to believe in or the God that I was still trying to let go of.

Tears must have dribbled down my cheeks on the trolley with the cot sides because a nurse was staring into my face.

'What are you thinking about?' she asked.

'Nothing,' I said. 'I just can't sleep.'

The following day, they gave me a lot of antibiotics
through a drip, so quickly that my arm began to tingle and sting. I was admitted to a ward, and lay behind blue curtains for most of the day, dizzy and confused, and enjoying only the regular interventions by nurses to check my temperature and blood pressure and ensure that the drip was dripping well. That night I was thirsty, but because I was going to have a colonoscopy in the morning, I couldn't take water. The nurse left a small stick the size of a toothpick with cotton wool on the end

of it beside a glass of water on the locker. 'Just rub your lips with it if you're thirsty,' she said. I thanked her.

'Your wife was very worried about you. She phoned a few minutes ago.'

'That's good to hear.'

'She must love you very much.'

'No,' I said, 'she doesn't love me at all. Nor I her. She thinks she loves me. And I thought I loved her. But that was all attachment. She wanted to make me happy. I wanted to make her happy. But what's that about? She does not love me and I love nobody.'

'You need to get some rest,' the nurse said.

The following morning, she came back with one of her mates and gave me an enema, which forced me into the toilet and the ward filled with smells of breakfast and smells from the loo. I was ashamed, but then they took me to theatre and did the colonoscopy, and all of a sudden it was the following day.

The surgeon stood at the foot of my bed and said, 'You have colitis.'

They sent me home with lots more antibiotics and tablets for settling my stomach, and steroids that I could inject through my own back passage. Every night I squirted the steroids up my bum with a syringe and a mirror to guide me, and I took my tablets obediently every three hours.

But I was developing a new problem. I could not move. My body was still as bad as it ever was. I knew everything had happened because I had overworked myself, and I felt stupid. It was like a punishment, and I felt I deserved it because I had been such an ass for most of my life.

Fr Fingers had made a comeback. He entered the room in a long black frock, with his canes and belts and books, with smoking pipe and funny hat and hairy eyebrows. The sterile mythic male who broke me in some ancient space and long ago was back and maybe now I would be locked away with him forever.

I didn't care that I had colitis. But I was ashamed. I lay there ashamed. Of everything. Ashamed of my diarrhoea. Ashamed of my enlarged prostate that was blocking my ability to pass water. Ashamed of God. Ashamed that I wrapped myself in religion for so many years only to discover that it was nothing more than insulation from depression and the grief of being mortal. Most of all, I was ashamed of being a man.

I had often met people who in old age or on their death bed had told me they no longer believed in God or an afterlife, but they kept quiet so as not to upset those who were grieving for their loss and who didn't fully appreciate the transient nature of human existence. But whether it's in society or in an individual, whether it is gradually over years or suddenly in trauma, the ebbing away of religious belief causes sorrow and loneliness, melancholy and depression.

And then something unexpected happened. One evening I went downstairs in my dressing gown and found my lady wife in the kitchen making pasta. It was just another ordinary day. Me upstairs wallowing in shame, self-pity and physical discomfort, riddled with infections and despairing about ever getting better. And her downstairs, making a dinner. It could have been a salad or a soup or any number of delicacies that she churned out in that kitchen and carried on a tray up the stairs to the sad bastard in the bed. But suddenly I saw her. I noticed her as I had not done for a long while. And I noticed that the dark-haired woman was turning grey.

In recent months, she had taken to the cigarettes for health reasons. She said it relaxed her, and helped her cope with the sick husband. She sat at the table folding loose tobacco into tiny strips of paper and then she slipped out the back to puff.

I went with her, and the two of us ended up standing there in the backyard looking at the sky, which was interesting because the swallows had built a new nest high up under the guttering, where the cat couldn't reach them. It was just finished, and we were both gawking up at it when she said, 'Is it swans that never part?'

'I've heard that said, but I don't know if it's true.'

'What about ducks?'

'Haven't a clue.'

'I think humans are more like ducks than swans.'

She was sucking the last of her little cigarette.

'Rolling cigarettes suits you,' I said. 'It gives a woman something to do, now that knitting has become unfashionable.'

We often played with each other like that.

'When you were in the hospital,' she said, 'I saw you waddling along the corridor one day, making that slithering noise with your slippers, and I said, "Yes, that's a duck."'

Then we went inside and sat at the table and drank a pot of green tea. After the conversation about the swans and the ducks there was nothing else to talk about. We sat in silence, waiting for the rice pudding to heat in the microwave, and it was just one of those evenings, when someone eventually breaks the silence by saying something like, *Why don't we go and look at the lake?* It's the kind of thing people said years ago, when they had nothing to do. Married couples, with little excitement in their lives, and missing the children who had scattered to the farthest corners of the globe, would often finish their rice pudding and look at each other and say, *Why don't we go and look at the lake?* Not that I was a fly on the wall of every house, but when I was young I saw enough people sitting in their cars at various lakeshores, staring out the window, and so I presumed such things. I presumed they had no wild adventures ahead of them, like I had. And maybe in my heartless youth, I had little sympathy for them.

My father lived in the drawing room, with his newspaper, quietly separated from my mother, who rarely sat down and was always washing something under the tap in the kitchen, but I know their existence was nevertheless symbiotic, because every five minutes he would go down to the kitchen to tell her something he had read in the paper, or ask her opinion on such national issues as the blowing up of Nelson's Pillar, or the legalisation of contraceptives, and she would say, 'I can't answer you now, I'm trying to wash the carrots.'

And there are people who still live in such conjoined balance that their names are never spoken except as pairs; Tom and Maureen, Lynn and Harry, Mary and Seán. The roads of Ireland are full of little cars, going to and from health centres and supermarkets and social welfare offices with old swans. Young people don't see love like that, in terms of two people depending on each other. At least I didn't.

So it's funny, being at the dinner table, finishing the rice pudding and hearing the beloved say, 'Why don't we go and look at the lake?' As if now it was our time to be doing such things. Now that the Leaving Certificate is over, and now that our daughter has launched herself into a new world, the lake beckons us. So off we went. She and me, silent and bewildered, after years of companionship. And we sat in her car, staring out the window at the blue of the water, the reeds glimmering in the evening sunlight, and the ducks. There's always ducks, comical and elegant, calling out across the lake the hoarse song of their being.

'I'm a duck,' I said. 'And you're a duck.'

I couldn't say what I meant but we had a lovely evening, just looking at the lake. And we didn't say much, because after twenty-five years there's nothing much to say. And yet it was extraordinary. As if a new horizon out there beckoned us, with things we had never, until that moment, imagined.

Part Two

In the bleak midwinter

I hadn't realised that things were so bad, until I ended up in hospital, sitting in a wheelchair, drinking a jug of pink liquid and waiting to be wheeled into a CT scanner. They wanted to find out if the blood coming from my back passage was a sign that I had bowel cancer. It wasn't. I had colitis, a gross irritation of the bowel wall, probably caused in my case by an overuse of antibiotics. If I was lucky, it might be a one-off attack. If I wasn't, then I might have a debilitating condition for the rest of my life.

A nurse told me that the trauma of sudden illness could sometimes induce depression. And so it did.

In the months that followed, my usual melancholy transformed into a swamp of sorrow, an ocean of grief, oozing from the pores of my skin, and constricting me in what strung-out jazz musicians might call 'the blues'.

At the end of July Cathy brought me home to Leitrim in my own jeep, like a broken Don Quixote, where I began recuperating, surrounded by windmills in the hills above Lough Allen. All day I sat in a chair on the patio and stared at the lake and the shoreline. The dishwasher was still in the kitchen, and Cathy still filled it to bursting point before putting it on, but it didn't seem important to me anymore. In fact, nothing seemed important as the leaves fell from the trees and autumn began to close in, apart from the fact that I woke up exhausted each morning, unable to get out of bed and dreading any encounter with other human beings.

Each evening I waited for darkness to descend. For supper I poured myself a bowl of cornflakes and drenched them with milk and sugar. I brushed my teeth, folded my shirt on the back of the chair and lay down on the bed. By then, it was already dark outside. Sometimes the neighbours' dog barked. Clouds drifted across the mountain, bringing rain that pelted the roof and reminded me that I was in Leitrim. Sometimes I rose and sat by the window, my head boiling, my body hot and foggy, my bladder full and yet unable to entirely empty and I'd sit there almost overwhelmed by the vastness of the obscure universe beyond the clouds. And it was then, at night, that the obscure universe within me also made its' presence felt; a formless black hole, churning and swelling like an ocean. For me, the ground of all being was black. And it was that blackness I waited for, while the rest of the house was sleeping. Even during the day, I was ambushed by sadness; it gnawed at my emotions, like a demonic bird come from the deep to pluck me to pieces.

I joined a leisure centre with Cathy in a local hotel and we drove to it every evening. I'd splash about, trying to swim, and sometimes I got weak in the sauna. Cathy insisted that exercise would help and I didn't disagree.

To cheer myself up, I went to see the Pulitzer Prize-winning poet Paul Muldoon reading poems in The Dock in Carrick-on-Shannon in late July. He was wearing a linen jacket over a black v-neck sweater, and he was a bit like a bird himself as he darted about the room, from one poem to another, his long hair falling in a mop of curls over the same bright and brilliant forehead that I had first seen almost thirty years earlier in Sligo at the Yeats Summer School.

In those days, Muldoon didn't dart about; he just stood intensely still at the podium, in a suit and tie, his fringe falling over his spectacled eyes, as the audience sat on bean bags and leaned against the wall, because it was fashionable back then to spurn anything as bourgeois as a chair. But

169

Muldoon looked well after all the years; a bit plump in the tummy but lighter in himself as he pronounced each lovely word as if he had just invented it.

The reading was an absolute pleasure, and I left the building content, but as soon as I drove home, and for no apparent reason, the ocean of misery inside me threw up black beaky demons again to shred my peace of mind. I couldn't explain it, or fathom the reason, but any ordinary moment of pleasure, like listening to poetry or buying an ice-cream cone at a filling station, could be suddenly flittered away by the savage presence of inner sadness.

On the first week in August, Frank arrived. A small squat man in his late sixties, he was married to Cathy's sister, and she asked him to help us put in a stove in a room that looked out on the patio and was rarely used in winter. Having a stove in it would give us much-needed extra space in the small cottage. It took him two days, so he stayed overnight and went to the pub with Cathy. I heard them return and make sandwiches in the kitchen, and I envied Frank his health and cheerfulness as I watched him the following morning eating a hearty breakfast before Cathy drove him to the train station.

Shortly after Frank had put in the stove, Cathy's brother Tom arrived from London for a few days, with bottles of an ale called Bishops Finger. At almost seventy, he was in poor health and he sat on a rocking chair on the patio for two days with a rug around him, because he smoked a lot and he didn't want to smoke in the house. For many years, he had worked in the office of a factory that produced asbestos and his lungs were destroyed, and to come home on the ferry had been a big effort. But he wanted to sit in the hills above Lough Allen with his sister, perhaps one last time, and look down at the shoreline where he and his father had once spent a splendidly happy day.

'I can still remember the sandwiches we ate at the waterside that afternoon,' he said.

He struggled for breath and stared at the lake and smoked his cigarettes in silence, and I wondered what flock of birds was eating his heart out, or what ocean of black terror awaited him every night.

I asked him if he slept well, and he just said, 'I was up every hour.'

When he was leaving, he walked to the taxi on his own, gripping his walking stick, with a rug still draped over his shoulders. It was obvious that he wouldn't last much longer. He bid me a last farewell with his raised hand as the car drove away and all evening I sat by the stove and looked out the patio door at the empty chair, rocking slightly in the breeze, and I saw a big crow land on the chair and turn its head sideways and gawk at me through the glass, just like an old friend.

Some nights I examined myself in the toilet. I spent hours evaluating my stool, my water and my general complexion in the mirror. Not that there was anything remarkable about my body, it was more or less the same as anyone else's. I was six foot tall. I had the usual appendages and accoutrements and orifices that you might expect on the body of a male human from this neck of the European woods at this particular time in history. From an anthropological point of view, I was as textbook a specimen as any ant. Except that I was bigger than an ant. And I had hair in my nostrils and in my ears and under my arms and on my lower body. The muscles on my upper arms and chest had withered and my flesh was as white as a sheet in a mortuary. I had no muscle left to speak of. I was a skeleton with flabby skin. The male organ looked as sad as a dead hen's neck. I would run my finger over my back and underarms looking for blotches, moles or other carbuncles that might be cancerous. I examined my scrotum which looked like a bag of worms, with purple veins bulging here and there under the skin, and I made a general assessment of the smell. Not just the smell of cock and piss, but the general body smell. And the taste in my mouth. All things about me seemed to reek of death.

Sometimes when a young woman got into the pool at the leisure centre, her perfume would hover over the water for a few moments and swimming through it was delicious, and I wondered if the opposite was the case with me. Did I leave behind me everywhere a scent that other people found repulsive?

But no matter how long I spent examining myself, I was never going to find the cause of my despair, because my wounds were all on the inside. Colitis was on the inside. The enlarged prostate that blocked me from urinating was on the inside. Though even these were bearable afflictions. The core problem was my negative mind. I would stare at myself in the mirror and accuse myself of having fucked up. I told myself that even the spiders in the bath were happy compared to me. Eventually they achieved their full potential. They all got out of the bath and made webs on the ceiling in the corners. Whereas I had failed. And the ultimate failure was the failure of the body. I couldn't stay out of bed for more than a few hours. In the sauna, I couldn't stay more than five minutes. I couldn't piss. I couldn't eat. And I couldn't think without being overwhelmed by negative emotions. I had failed at everything. I was a failed husband, a failed priest and a failed writer. The list was as endless as the night was long, and the image in the mirror did not disagree with me.

173

As a teenager, I had shaken my guts out for years to the sound of the showbands in dance halls around Cavan and Longford. It was my only option in an unconscious world, though even then I fancied that my body glided around the slippery floors with the grace of Rudolf Nureyev or the carnality of John Travolta. And for years I harboured the delusion that my feet and toes were as pretty as a little girl's – until I took off my sock one night at a party and the girl

I was with screamed in horror. I flailed away in the gym for years to avoid a beer belly until an older man laughed at me one day in the dressing room when he caught me glancing at myself sideways in the mirror. 'I think you've lost,' he said. And so I had.

But it's hard to believe that I could lie awake for hours, envying John Travolta or a Russian ballet dancer and the spiders in the bath. And since it would be hard to believe that someone could actually stand before a mirror for hours in the middle of the night, nursing a kind of irrational contempt for his own body and for his life's history, I never told anyone what was going on.

'How did you sleep?' Cathy would enquire in the morning.

'Ah, not too bad,' I'd reply.

When I was in bed, I clung to the pillow. I clung to an old vest, as if it were a worry blanket and I was a child in my cot and my mother's face was a great moon above me, shining down on me. Sometimes I would visualise the face of the old Tibetan Lama in west Cavan with whom I had studied ten years earlier and sometimes that helped me sleep. But if I did sleep, it was only for an hour or so. Even on moonless nights, when a heavy blanket of cloud and rain smothered Leitrim in a dark damp stillness, I couldn't sleep. I would greet the dawn wide awake as I lay there exhausted, still surfing across memories of life in Mullingar, and the fun and excitement of being on the road with a theatre show, and my unrelenting quest for love in random Centra stores; a life that had crashed to smithereens in a few weeks and left me in despair.

In the spring of 2011, when the tour of *The Tinker's Curse* was in full swing, I was invited on to a radio programme in Dublin to promote the show. I remember seeing a mink on my way to the train that morning; black and shiny, it's gorgeous coat far superior to even the most beautiful black cat I ever had. It was running across the road that leads down to Lough Ennell, where the swans live. There was something about its wild nature that I envied.

That night, I was on the radio with two other people; a young man and a woman, both of whom are known as entertainment journalists. We were going to talk about movies.

When the programme began, I tried to sound as if I knew something about Hollywood.

'Apparently Sandra Bullock is having personal problems,' I declared, but everybody already knew that.

The young man beside me explained how the movie under review was not very good and was the same as half a dozen other movies and how the storyline was silly, but that Sandra looked good.

'If you like Sandra,' he said, 'you will like this.'

He sounded as if he knew her intimately.

The presenter was just off a plane from New York and he was sporting an impressive tan. The young woman on the panel was all giggles, like Marilyn Monroe, on the verge of ecstasy, as if this was the happiest day of her life.

I just didn't know enough about movies, and I couldn't keep up with the eloquence of the other two. I was amazed by how much they knew about celebrities and by all the hot gossip they had about Hollywood. At one stage, I asked them if there was any danger that we might be losing the run of ourselves, and that perhaps our over-familiarity with American culture was a sign that we were, as a nation, still colonised. They looked at me as if I had two heads. I left the studio a bit dazed and wandered into a nearby pub. A young woman in gothic evening wear was leaning against the bar and holding her head, like she had a migraine. I asked her if anything was wrong. She said she'd been in the back of a taxi and she'd heard an old geezer on the radio trying to say something intelligent about movies.

'The old fart probably wasn't at a movie for decades,' she said. 'He was going on about being colonised or something. He said he was from Mullingar, wherever that is! Probably on planet Zog!'

'No,' I said. 'Mullingar is in Westmeath. It's an hour away on the train.'

'How do you know?' she asked.

'The fart on the radio was me.'

'Jesus,' she exclaimed, 'that's cool.'

We didn't have much of a vocabulary in common, so I tried to use words judiciously.

When she asked me if I would like to join her for a drink, I said, 'That would be cool.'

And then the drinks arrived – my wine and her vodka – which is when she realised that she had left her money in the taxi. She was all distressed about that, so I paid, and she thanked me and I said, 'Don't worry, it's cool.'

Then for the sake of conversation, I said that I had seen a sleek black mink that morning, on the road to Lough Ennell where the swans live and that it was utterly wild and beautiful. She stared at me with some unease, and said, 'You're really off the wall, man.' She said it without mercy or humour.

'I know,' I said. 'I know.'

She meant it, and I had a sense of foreboding at the time. That had only been a few months earlier. Now I was standing in the bathroom in Leitrim staring at the mirror. It was 3 a.m. 'Off the wall, man.' I knew now what she had meant.

I missed Mullingar. I felt exiled in Leitrim.

Mullingar was attractive. Sexy. I walked about in a state of bliss. I liked being in a town. Having lots of Centra and Spar shops to choose from. And supermarkets. And pubs. I liked having coffee in Café Le Monde in the Harbour Place Shopping Centre and watching all the people going in and out of Dunnes Stores. Mullingar was colourful. There were Poles and Russians. Chefs and solicitors. There were thousands of people. But in Leitrim, we lived up the hills. It was desolate. And by September the nights were getting shorter. Cathy said we should keep up the swimming. Swimming might bring me out of myself. So I agreed. But I was barely able for it. I told her I couldn't function because of the black feeling that pervaded my body sometimes.

'Maybe we're missing something,' she suggested.

She meant that I might need tablets. So I went to the doctor and the doctor said she could prescribe some if things got too bad, but I said that my brother knew a therapist in America who was going to talk to me on a Skype link, so I was OK for the moment. The doctor raised an eyebrow but made no comment.

In fact, the therapist was brilliant. I talked to him every week. Sometimes the image on the screen broke up and I would lose the connection and he'd phone me and we'd continue talking on the telephone. And my brother phoned every evening. There were lots of people around me all trying to help, but I was locked inside myself. And the pool in the leisure centre was underground with poor lighting and no windows and sometimes I felt worse coming out than I had going in. And then we drove home on dark, unlit roads through a wilderness of forestry and wind and flooded fields. And all the time I longed for Mullingar. I longed to see young people in vibrant clothes, like the Goths I used to watch from a seat in Café Le Monde as they loitered around the glass doors of mobile phone shops or boutiques selling cheap dresses. The only gothic animals

179

in Leitrim were the neighbours' dreadfully undernourished horses.

In Mullingar the Goths used to hang around McDonald's, the Harbour Place Shopping Centre and other public places, in their black coats, their purple-mascara eyes and their long dreadlocks, weaved with red and black ribbons. Betimes, the girls had noses like pincushions and open black shirts with red vests beneath.

I used to fantasise that they might stab me with syringes of hallucinogenic drugs, and take me away and force me to have sex or sacrifice me on a makeshift altar under a full moon, with a broken Smirnoff bottle. Goths were formal outsiders. A glamorous post-punk critique of the bland and passionless 'cool' in modern Celtic Tiger Ireland. Their corsets and safety pins were an unconscious cry for something metaphysical. Their boots and buckles were a manifesto of faith in other worlds, woven in the grammar of fashion. They were philosophers in performance; the existential despair that had rattled Europe fifty years earlier still rippled in their mutilated faces and in their black nails and purple lipstick, and the rings and things that pierced their noses, eyebrows, ears and bellies. But they were always full of surprises. I remember two females of the species pushing their trolley along the meat aisle in Tesco one day. I expected them to speak in Latin or with the gravity of Count Dracula but instead they were yapping away in the soft buttery accents of Westmeath.

'It doesn't matter.'

'I know.'

'I mean it doesn't.'

'I know.'

'I mean he's an ee-gah.'

'I know.'

'I mean, it's not as if you said anything to him.'

'I know.'

'It's not as if you were running after him.'

'Yeah, I know.'

'You were only inviting him.'

'Jesus, I know.'

'Jesus. I mean you're entitled to invite who you like.'

'Jesus, shut up.'

They were both examining a Polish sausage.

'I wouldn't eat that! Would you?'

'No.'

'What d'ya do with it?'

'Boil it, I think.'

Their laughter made me shiver with loneliness, and I picked up a quick-fry steak and pushed on towards the hardware aisle. I was looking for a salad bowl that day and I thought Tesco would have a salad bowl. They had everything else. They had cutlery, saucepans, smoothie makers, microwaves, Pyrex dishes and roasting trays. But not a salad bowl in sight. And then I saw one of those frying pans that have high sides, and I put it in my trolley, convinced that I needed it. I came for a salad bowl, but I went home with a frying pan and two saucepans. That's what was wonderful about Mullingar in the time of the Tiger. It had everything.

Admittedly, for the first few months in Mullingar, I had been sad and homesick, and I had been uneasy about leaving Cathy and losing my home in the hills. But I soon got used to the midlands town. It was a cool spot, especially at weekends. There was an urban beat. A glittering show passing before me as I sat on a bar stool and gazed out at the world.

The first weekend I was there, I went to the Yukon Bar and heard an old folk singer singing one of his own songs in a dark voice, which reminded me of lonesome hobos staring out through the wooden slits of boxcars in Louisiana. And at the same gig, I saw a long-haired Polish boy perform. He stood at the mike, between two speakers, plucking his guitar. His eyes closed, not trying to connect with anyone. As if he was alone in some empty space and far away. That was cool! Mullingar was cool. Definitely cool.

Tuxedos and cocktail dresses were not uncommon in the lounge of Danny Byrne's when the good times were rolling. Everyone cruising the pubs, the clubs, the off-licence, the music venues and even along the banks of the Royal Canal. And you could always expect to see the Goths in unexpected places. Expect to see a girl in commando boots who would make a German dominatrix proud, leaning against the wall of some back alley. Goths were erotic terrorists. Hidden away in the shadows of the urban. Like shreds of remorse in an untended soul. They called to me. Sirens in the alleyway, and me a middle-aged man. What was that about? Surely it was the writing on the wall.

I suppose the truth is that I didn't take advantage of the urban chaos when I was young and virile. Or maybe I just didn't trust women back then and now, in middle age, I was running around a town in the midlands of Ireland like Don Quixote on Valium. I was frustrated by all the adventures I'd never had as a young man. I never got into bed with Goths or punks back then. I was reared on country and western music.

I remember when I was twenty-two, I bought a grey Austin A40 with a mahogany dashboard, and drove it up into the mountains of west Cavan. I abandoned suburbia, and crossed into a world where everyone was heroic and each deed was epic and the enormous mountain gripped every insignificant creature in a savage and mythic embrace. While others worked out their existential angst in urban flats, wallowing in the metaphysics of Leonard Cohen, I was quick-stepping around Glangevlin Hall or listening to Charley Pride in the middle of the night in cosy kitchens and country farmhouses. I would go out on the lawn to smoke Albany cigarettes because, outside, the moonlit mountain was magnificent, and I felt cousin to the goats bleating on the rocks and the badgers that waddled the roads unhindered by any combustion engine. The love songs of shy girls, the heroic recitations of daft old men with alcoholic noses glowing pink, and the long winter nights full of riddles, conundrums and *The Best of Hank Williams* seduced my heart. It was a labyrinth of fun, from which there was little chance of recovery.

And so in later life, I sometimes wandered around Mullingar like Prospero, shipwrecked in the drab modernity of the New Ireland, momentarily bored with teenage Goths and sometimes feeling desperate for a good jive.

They were still jiving in the Greville Arms Hotel on Sunday nights when I arrived in Mullingar in 2006, in a wonderfully faded ballroom, with elegance reminiscent of Fred Astaire, dancing in black and white on the Sunday afternoon television of my childhood. A mannered world of chandeliers, wigs, flashy jackets, and well-shod ladies in trouser suits, gold necklaces and strong mascara. In the quiet corners, softly lit, grey-haired old men opened their hearts in whispered conversation with women who had been waiting for decades. An intimate tiptoe time, as delicate as a foxtrot. Though some dancers were old, and their bodies sagged, there was a weightlessness in their expressions. The singers wore suits of blue. And everyone was full of expectation.

One night, I sat in the din and the glare, admiring a mature lady on the dance floor with pride in her stride and a little too much rouge in her cheeks. She tilted her head back. She couldn't give a damn. And boy could she jive, on the floor of the Greville Arms Hotel.

A woman asked me was I ever in the Marquee in Drumlish.

I replied, 'I think that's the title of a song.'

'Oh, by jingo it is,' she said, her eyes wistful, and watering. 'It's a song all right.'

Then Texas came up in conversation.

'D'ye know,' she said, 'if I got the chance to go to Texas, I'd never come back.'

I wondered why. At first she couldn't say. She thought about it.

'The horses maybe,' she said. 'The horses.'

I asked her if she remembered the Hank Williams song about a horse.

A terrible disappointment flooded into her eyes, and she said, 'No. No, I never liked Hank Williams.' And then she drifted away.

185

The boy to my left leaned towards me and said, 'I heard ye quizzing yer wan about Texas.'

'Yes,' I said. 'We were just chatting.'

'Well,' he said, 'I've got every single song Hank Williams ever recorded.'

He looked me in the eye and began to sing 'I'm so lonesome I could cry'.

He winked at me and added, 'D'ye know what I'm saying?', before he walked away.

And then at last, fortified by Guinness and in thrall to the glittering lights, I agreed to dance.

'Listen,' she said, 'forget about Hank Williams. I'm asking ye, can ye jive?'

I was about to say no, but I could hear a voice, whispering, '*Yes. Yes of course I could jive.*'

'*And quick step as well,*' said the ghost at my shoulder in the Greville Arms Hotel.

And so finally, after long years of maturity and rational thought as a husband, father and mediocre flute player in Leitrim, I let go again in Joe Dolan's country. And into an ocean of perfume, across a sea of buckskin shirts, I jived with a stranger. A lovely lady who reminded me of nobody in particular. And when we were finished, she said, very demurely, that I jived rather well.

So I had a lot to talk about every week on the Skype link to New York with my Gestalt therapist as I brought him up to speed with fifty years of my childhood days in Ireland. And I had a lot to think about as I lay in bed, day after day, until noon.

I'd eat a lunch with Cathy and sometimes go back to bed for another hour, dreaming again. And she would nurse me. Enclose me. Enfold me. My wife became a mother, and gave me time to weep. She gave me space to mourn. She bore witness to my shame and my childish tears as I gripped her hand and begged her not to leave me alone in the dark.

The colitis cleared up. But I was chronically depressed and physically exhausted, and other bits of my body were breaking down at regular intervals.

One night I couldn't pass any water at all. I was awake the entire night, in pain, coming and going to the bathroom without success. I was terrified. I felt my bladder was going to explode. By morning I was desperate. So Cathy drove me back to the hospital in Mullingar and after some heroic mechanical work by the nurses, the problem was fixed. But the prostate had become so enlarged that they suggested an operation to shrink it. And since I was too ill from the colitis and exhaustion to endure such a procedure at that stage, they said I should wait until the new year and that I should take Omsil tablets in the meantime.

The Omsil tablets probably prevented me from seizing up entirely, but I was walking around with a half-full bladder all the time even when I'd finished in the toilet. It didn't help cheer me up.

On another occasion, Cathy drove me to the doctor in Ballyfarnon. She sat outside in the car as I sat inside in a tiny waiting room with country people and a small transistor radio that was blaring cowboy music into everyone's grim faces. The doctor suggested antidepressants. I left, and Cathy drove me home again.

I went back to bed for the afternoon and she put on a wash. Every day she drove to a supermarket in town and bought two takeaway dinners. And as the leaves turned yellow on the chestnut and beech trees at the end of August and the evenings got shorter, she put on fires and we sat in silence, looking across the room at each other, wondering what might happen next. Depression seemed like something that could never end.

I would say, 'I don't think it will end.'

And she would say, 'Of course it will end. Trust me.'

And like a child I did. She was giving me time to mourn and to cry for all the lives that I had never lived. Before I let them go.

Sickness emasculates a man. And as the autumn wrapped itself around our little cottage with fallen leaves and harsh winds and endless squalls of rain from the west, my life revolved around a simple lunch each day and a trip to the leisure centre with Cathy, and a mug of Marmite going to bed. And I felt emasculated. Not that I ever thought of myself as much of a man in the first place. I never played football growing up or watched sports as an adult. And my adventures in Mullingar were a sort of mid-life crisis. A desperate attempt to be a hunter at last.

I remember the autumn of 2006, shortly after I had arrived in Mullingar. I was sitting on a bench in the railway station with a ticket for Dublin, and thinking about the ozone layer. I must have looked depressed, because a man in an anorak and a sensual lower lip smiled straight at me.

'It beats driving up the motorway,' he said. He was talking about the Dublin train. 'You can leave before nine, scrum in the aisles all day long, and be back on the platform at Mullingar not long after six. I have a jeep,' he confessed, 'but I never use it.'

'The jeeps are heavy on the juice,' I said.

'You're not long in Mullingar,' said anorak man, taking out a Silvermint to suck with his sensual mouth, arranging himself on the bench, and making me fear that he might stick to me for the entire trip to Connolly Station.

'No,' I admitted, 'I'm new in town.'

He sucked the mint and stared out into the middle distance like a detective.

'So what do you think of it so far?' he whispered.

'So far so good,' I said, 'except that people drive very zippy up and down the streets and around the roundabouts.'

'What are you driving?' he wondered.

'A Ford Ka—' I started to confess.

'Ah, for frig sake!' he said. 'The wife has one of them yokes!'

And he walked off down the platform to the front of the train before I could finish my sentence.

A few weeks later, I bought a Mitsubishi Pajero. On the one hand, I thought my hunting days were over, because I was in my fifties, but, on the other, I thought Mullingar might be a new beginning. And a jeep seemed to be essential for the hunter in the lush land of horses and heifers and well-heeled ladies on Celtic Tiger patios.

I was taking my first spin in the Pajero and was just beyond the toll plaza one day when I saw a girl hitching.

'Where are you going?' she asked.

'Dublin,' I said.

She hopped in, which delighted me, even though the jeep was full of used tissues and empty Coke bottles. There was even an old vest on the passenger seat, which I managed to fling into the back before she noticed.

'I'm giving a workshop to young writers this afternoon,' I said. I thought that would impress her. But she said nothing until we reached the quays.

'Drop me at Capel Street,' she announced and I did. She was gone without as much as a smile in my direction. An hour later, I was walking up Abbey Street, after parking in the Irish Life Centre, and was still disappointed that even with a Pajero I didn't seem to be visible to the female of the species. Out of habit, I looked in a shop window, to check my appearance, and suddenly I wished I was invisible. My hair was standing up in a bushy heap. Clearly nobody would take me seriously at a workshop if I arrived with a head looking like a tuft of rushes. So I went to a chemist and bought Brylcreem, and then went into the men's toilet in the Gresham Hotel and massaged my head with the white cream, in the hope of improving the overall image. I felt like Marilyn French, the great feminist, who once had an epiphany in a rest room as she made up her face to be presentable to men.

A man came into the toilet and stared at me with some pity as I worked frantically at the mirror.

He grinned, and said, 'Whoever she is, son, she's not worth it!'

I said, 'Actually, it's not a woman. It's just that I'm meeting a lot of people in a few minutes and I want to look my best. And quite honestly, to look your best, you have to feel your best and, after listening to Marian Finucane all morning, I don't feel very good at all; so I need the Brylcreem. Does that make sense?'

He relieved himself, as real men do, with the force of a camel whose bladder has not been emptied for weeks, and then he left the room without even giving his forefingers a ritual rinse under the tap. I put the Brylcreem in my briefcase and headed off for the workshop.

The Pajero was fifteen years old and not in great condition. I was parked just down from the dog track one day when a young fellow with a smooth hairless face pulled up beside me in a blazing red Toyota. His window opened.

He shouted at me, 'You'll get a right wallop in the arse there, if you're not careful.'

I said, 'I beg your pardon?'

He said, 'You've no light at the back!'

'Where did you get her?' he asked. (He called my Pajero a her!)

'In a garage.'

He said, 'She's clean, for a ninety-three.' But, he explained, 'You need to go to a man on the Kilbeggan Road. He'll sort ye. He's behind the Centra.'

'I'll do that,' said I. And I did.

Mullingar had roundabouts, motorway bypasses and car parks, all haunted by shadowy packs of young men. Boys in saloon cars with the windows blacked out – bangers dressed up with spoilers and mufflers. They hunt by night and have no time for the world of safety or speed limits. They are prisoners of Love and Mythos, and a future that never stretches beyond the next dawn. But I couldn't help liking them. Young Turks, Balubas, call them what you want, in some places when the jeeps roll into the car park of a pub, the older clients are heard to whisper, 'Here comes the Taliban!'

It was a young lad fixed my jeep. Opened up the back light unit and exposed a spaghetti bowl of wires to my ignorant eyes and pointed to a yellow one and said, 'D'ye see that yellow one?'

I did.

'Well,' he said, 'that shouldn't be there. That's your fogs. Shouldn't be wired in there at all. Every time you turn on the fog lights, you blow the fuse for the tails and dash.'

I wanted to be like those young lads cruising through the night with a battery of four beams blinding the eyes of oncoming traffic. He looked at me. Made a quick judgement about age and said, 'Sure you don't need fog lights, do you?'

'I suppose I don't,' I said. 'There's hardly much need for fog lights at my age.'

That night I walked up to Dominick Street for chips. I asked for a large chip. But instead the young Italian boy gave me two singles because he hadn't understood what I'd said. When I pointed out the mistake he said sorry. And then he said I could have both bags for the same price.

On the street outside, the alloy wheels were spinning and the engines were purring as a few young men cruised into the night. They were probably heading out the Dublin road towards the Park Hotel, glowing as it does like some *Titanic* in the dark. Out across the long stretches of flat tarmac road along the straight double lanes all the way to the toll plaza, feeling nomadic in those sweet hours of the night. *They are hunters of love, booze and chips*, I thought, *depending what hour of the night it is. They swarm through the dark and land in the car parks of nightclubs or cinemas with the grace of geese, and just a hint of threat.* Wild geese. Warriors hunting under a full moon. Believing in some goddess to keep them safe on the road home. To keep them cool when speeding and taking risks and showing off. Rubber burning on the tar. The boys at the wheel,

194

burning with a passion for the hunt that I had long ago mislaid.

In the years I spent in Mullingar, the nearest I got to being a warrior hunter was when I went to Dublin occasionally for an overnight and stayed in some city hotel and fished around the bar for an hour or two looking for company. I remember one night in January 2010, I was staying in Ballsbridge because I was on a radio show the following morning. The hotel was full of students in school uniforms, from every corner of the country, mingling in frenzied chaos, sitting on the stairs, huddling around the soft drinks machine and ogling each other as they engaged in flirtatious chatter. Some even sat in a circle on the floor of the foyer, while one of them sang and played a guitar, and those who listened were like dazed sheep, enraptured by the beauty of the song and the gaze of strangers. For a man of my years, the sight of young people wandering about in a fog of unfocused lust can be an unsettling experience. I began humming 'Forever Young' by Bob Dylan as I checked in. I took off my glasses because I don't think I look very cool with glasses, and I was trying desperately to be cool, amid the throng of frisky youths. The receptionist was confused because I had filled in my name on the wrong line.

195

'Please,' she said, 'put your name here, on this line.' She fingered the correct spot.

I said, 'I'm sorry, I don't have my glasses with me.'

She looked at me and said, 'They're on your head.'

Then I walked to the lift, pulling my suitcase behind me with the sophisticated swagger of an airline pilot heading for the VIP lounge after landing an Airbus, and trying to suck in my potbelly so that I didn't look too absurd. The teenagers around me were giddy, and when I squashed myself into the lift with nine of them, I felt like a bull in a china shop and I feared I might be asphyxiated in a cloud of perfume.

Later, in the bar, I met a woman in a green dress with an identity badge hanging around her neck, as if she was a security person in an airport. She was about forty, had a ponytail, the remains of a beautiful face and an air of hope in her eyes.

She said, 'Who are you with?'

I said, 'I'm on my own.'

'Sorry,' she said, 'I thought you were with one of the other schools.'

I said, 'I presume they're all young scientists.'

'Correct,' she said, and she laughed and agreed to join me for a drink.

'Do you know,' she said later, 'that an earwig looks like a butterfly, except he has no wings? Everyone loves a butterfly, but the earwig must feel sad that nobody loves him.'

'Is that something scientific?' I wondered.

'No,' she said, 'it's just me being silly.'

All of a sudden, I began wondering where this was going, and a little part of me dared speculate on the possibilities.

196

Could it be that this was the moment I had been waiting for all my life? The moment that all men dream of? The night when anonymous ships go bump, secure in the knowledge that both participants are nice people with clean minds and healthy bodies? I'd often heard rumours about moments of passion that can occur among members of staff on school outings, at union conferences or during Alcoholics Anonymous weekends. And she wore no wedding ring, and she was maybe forty and so I asked her did she like Bob Dylan. She just said, 'Ahhh, 'Forever Young'!'

She clinked her glass of wine against my pint. My heart was palpitating. So I excused myself and headed for the men's room where I had a little chat with myself and tried to calm down. Banish any moral misgivings! I told my other self in the mirror; time enough for morality in the morning!

'Soooo, tell me about yourself,' I said, when I returned.

'I live with my mother,' she declared. For some reason, that's where it all ended. The flirtation was suspended. She said she was exhausted from working with young people. 'They have too much energy,' she said, 'it just drains me. And then I go home and look after my mum.'

We spent some more time at the bar discussing various other topics as wholesome as the digestive biscuits I used to nibble during charismatic prayer meetings years earlier when I was lonely and yearned for intimacy and the possibility of weeping with women, without being disturbed by sexual

197

desires. When she was going, she brushed her lips against my beard and said, 'You have sad eyes.'

'So will you have,' I replied, 'when you're my age.'

I watched her leave the lounge, her lovely green dress swishing as she walked. But as far as the bright young people in the foyer were concerned, she was as invisible as I was, which I suppose has everything to do with Mother and staying too long in her shadow.

There were other moments. Brief encounters that led round in circles in dozens of other hotels. But I just didn't see who I was becoming. And I didn't understand why I was getting more and more depressed and lonely as I roamed the countryside with my one-man theatre show. From Kerry to Donegal I played small arts venues, parish halls, festivals and hotel function rooms. I talked on local radio, pretended I was famous, distributed my own flyers and put up my own posters, and then warmed up for the afternoon, rested for an hour or so and stepped into the limelight to pour my heart and soul onto the floor in front of strangers.

It was both exhilarating and exhausting. It was a blessing and a curse. I stayed in different hotels. I moved about the country like a shadow. I loved the anonymity of those small country hotels, places where I could be both close to other people and yet utterly aloof. Just as mediaeval monks paced their cloisters, I paced hotel foyers, and I was close to other people without being intimate.

In hotels I wrapped myself in solitude, as I stood in the lift or sauna or lounge bar. It was as if at last I were a ghost in the world of others. At night I heard people wallowing through orgasms in distant rooms, just as a dying person might hear children playing outside a window. Eventually I sat in the sauna with equanimity and without desire, no matter who was sitting on the other bench. I was at home in the poverty of my own bones. So a good hotel was about the only degree of intimacy I could bear, especially after being on stage all evening. To know that there was love out there beyond the wall was enough. And to know that where I slept, I was safe from harm.

As the September days grew shorter and the nights stretched longer, I was getting out of bed more often and I had more energy when the time came for my regular check-ups with the doctor. I always had a good soak whenever I had an appointment with the doctor, because I never knew what part of my anatomy was going to come under scrutiny. I was following small routines and becoming resigned to a future of infirmity. The daughter began First Arts in Galway and the house we rented in Mullingar was emptied, and the keys handed back to the landlord. My little adventure for five years beyond the scope of my wife was over. But I didn't feel emasculated anymore. I knew I needed her, and was able to admit it for the first time in my life. I said it to my brother one day on the phone and he said, 'You sound vulnerable.'

'Do I?' I was surprised.

'Yes,' he said. 'You sound vulnerable for the first time in your life.'

And it was a good feeling. If there was one thing I had learned from talking to the therapist on the Skype link to America, it was that there is nothing in life to be ashamed of. To be sick or old or less than perfect or in need of help is simply human. To be vulnerable is human. And the shame that keeps us silent and makes men wear a warrior's shield at all times and pretend to be invincible is something less than human. Shame and silence make men into caricatures of humanity that crash in middle age and die alone. I was beginning to read my illness with a new mind. Maybe I was beginning to get somewhere. But I had a long way to go.

It was almost 6 p.m. when I got to the doctor's waiting room one wet evening in late September for my regular check-up, and the radio was on. Matt Cooper was asking the presidential candidates if they believed in God, but the radio wasn't tuned properly to the station, so it was impossible to hear any answers. An old man turned to me

201

and said, 'I'm glad to see you out. We heard you had taken to the bed.'

'Not the bed,' I said. 'The stove. I have taken to the stove. And the lake. I look at the lake a lot.'

Years ago people suffering from depression often took to the bed, because houses were damp and there was no central heating and there was no peace to be had in the kitchen because it was an industrial zone; kettles sang on the range, women peeled potatoes, drying sheets hung like flags from the rafters, and children picked their noses under the table and tried to learn Irish words from schoolbooks.

So if a man wanted to fall into the soft silence of his own psyche for a couple of years and escape the intellectual paralysis of the new Free State, he took to the bed. If a woman, after years of childbearing and washing nappies, wanted to escape the emotional wilderness of rural Ireland in the rain, she took to the bed. The bed was the warmest place to be alone and to rest, away from the turmoil of being Irish or married or both. It was either that or stand in the turf shed and stare out at the rain for years or contemplate some watery end in the local river.

Nowadays people can afford to heat more than just a kitchen, so when a person wants to escape the maddening world, they can go into another room and close the door. Each morning, I cleaned out my stove. I brushed the ashes onto a shovel and dropped them in a bucket. I filled a wicker basket with turf briquettes and placed the basket in the corner. I stood six briquettes inside the stove, mounted on a fire lighter, ready to be lit, whenever the urge took me. After that, my day could begin. Everything was possible.

Sitting at the stove was what my therapist called a safe place; a place where I could explore all sorts of exercises in mindfulness, as I lay on the couch. I could doze and listen to music, and even when old friends called I didn't feel I needed to fuss or make an effort. I just lay on the couch and smiled at them.

My dearest friend, the General, came to visit on 8 December. Cathy had gone to Dublin to shop and we sat by the open fire in the lounge for the entire afternoon, without exchanging a single word. The General is in his late sixties and I have referred to him for years as the General because of his seniority and authority.

And there he was in an armchair opposite me and a bunch of flowers, of all things, on his lap, on a cold December afternoon a few weeks before Christmas, and I didn't feel the slightest need to fuss or entertain him. I just dozed and daydreamed and wondered why we had remained such good friends over all the years. I wondered if the secret police knocked on the door would we cling to each other in loyalty or endure death camps together because of love. Because we all like to think of ourselves as heroes. We would all like to play Schindler in *Schindler's List*.

'I hope you're minding yourself,' the General said.

'*Schindler's List* was on the telly last night,' I said.

203

'Great to see the open fire,' he said.

I nodded and thought to myself that the General, too, is ageing. He that was mighty and once walked into any room with an arched back and a smile that said *Pay attention to me, ladies!* has no colour left in his face except the greyness of a watery twilight, as he stares across the flickering room at me, wondering if the woman who jilted him during the year might have been the last love of his life. Or is there more?

'There's always more,' I say.

The General's phone rang and though he was dozing by the fire, he bounced into life, became airborne as he reached for the mobile on the mantelpiece. It could be her, he whispered. It could be her; but it wasn't. So we fell back into reverie, and I daydreamed of a white Christmas, and the sun coming in through the glass of a hall door, as it used to when I was a child. I daydreamed of a white scarf some carol singer left abandoned on a bar stool years ago, and I could still recall the scent of it, and suddenly the General announced that a young man he knew had hanged himself during the week.

'In his own house,' the General said. 'His father found him and had to hold the poor boy aloft, but couldn't get him undone from the rope; he stood there in the hallway, propping up the unconscious boy so that his neck would not break, while he phoned the ambulance on his mobile.'

'Imagine …' said the General, '… in the hallway of a house he couldn't pay the mortgage on.'

I heard noises on the roof.

'What was that?' the General wondered.

'Angels,' I suggested.

Because I would still like to believe in angels above the rooftops in the dark, and because the darkness of midwinter could not possibly be all that there is. Could it?

The following morning I scooped ashes from the fire grate and heard crows cackling in the chimney, as if they had heard us the previous night and were still laughing. Cathy came home and found me at the television and the bed unmade. The fire wasn't cleaned out. The dishes were in the sink. The carpet in the lounge was covered in dust from turf briquettes.

She said, 'Maybe you need to get out on your own. Take the jeep and see if you can go for a spin somewhere.'

So I did. It was the first time I had ventured anywhere alone, and the first time I had sat behind the wheel of the jeep in months. I drove to Drumkeerin, through a street of closed-down shops. I drove towards Dowra where we used to leave the Labrador in kennels when the daughter was a child and we were going on holidays. By the time I got to Blacklion it was raining, and the clouds were purple over Lough MacNean and I didn't know where to go. So I just drove in a daze until I found myself in Derrylin, where I was once a priest, and I steered the jeep to the lough shore

205

near Aughakillymaude pier. I turned off the engine and walked a bit and looked out on the lake where I once had my own boat. That was in 1982.

I'd been heading off to shoot ducks on the shore of Lough Erne with a tall man called Mervin, who had bushy eyebrows and was passionate about little else in the world except duck-shooting. Mervin had lived on the shore and he took me into the woods behind his house and I had held the gun as he'd thrown a bucket in the air. I was supposed to wait until he'd shouted *Now*, so he could get out of the way. But I'd been thinking about something else and was too troubled to concentrate on the task in hand, and seeing the bucket move from his hand into the air I'd instinctively aimed and fired. Then Mervin had shouted a string of curses at me because he'd been able to hear the shot fly past his ears. 'Not so fast the next time,' he'd said when he had recovered, but for me there was no next time.

'I'm not going to win any prizes for shooting,' I'd declared, and he'd agreed.

'Maybe you'd make a better hand of the fishing?' he'd joked, and then he'd shown me a boat lying in his garage that he'd been trying to get rid of and, impulsively, I'd decided to buy it. An eighteen-foot slender vessel made of wood with two great oars. He'd talked about the fish in the lake. The eels that could be caught in the deep. The pike and the trout that lived in the reeds.

206

'You have more opportunities,' he'd said, 'when you have a boat.'

And he'd been right. I would never have met Celia Maguire if I hadn't had the boat. Celia Maguire was old but she was like me in a way. Because she was hunchbacked, she was always slightly ashamed of her body and as a result she ended up a recluse on an island in Lough Erne. After I got the boat I became friends with her. She'd grown up in a large family but she'd seen them all leave, her brothers and sisters, one by one, for husbands and wives on the mainland. She'd never married. A tiny girl with a deformed body, she may have found it difficult to attract suitors and had rarely been seen in public when she was young, except for Sunday mass. When her parents died, she'd pottered around for years on her own. On one occasion, a British army helicopter had flown overhead and the soldiers had seen smoke from her chimney, and suspected terrorists might be hiding on the island. They had landed and surrounded the house but she made them all tea and they flew away again. She'd made me tea too, on many occasions, when I sat with her and she'd told me stories about her life.

She told me of the night her house went on fire. And only by the quickness of her dogs did she wake up and crawl from her bed through the smoke and out the front door. There was no fire brigade to call. And there was no neighbour to call. So she sat in the bushes and watched the flames leap into the night and devour her little house. In the morning, a farmer on the mainland saw the black shell still smouldering. He alerted others and the news spread along the mainland and boats were floated from all over Fermanagh and there was consternation as they searched for her around the charred building. She was hiding in a cowshed, wearing only a threadbare cotton nightdress and ashamed to be seen.

'She would be far better off if she signed herself into a nursing home,' they said. But Celia dismissed that idea. So after a few days, they organised a flotilla of boats and cruisers, and ferried blocks and cement, timber and scaffolding, hammers and nails across the waters of the lough to rebuild her home.

The night the building was finished they took in crates of porter, and beer and bottles of whiskey and fiddles and flutes, and they played music and danced round her kitchen till the early hours. The sun was already high in a blue sky as the party ended and everyone went to the water's edge, each to their own boat, and headed back for the mainland. They were shook and hung over, and they marvelled at the water all around them. It seemed like being in another world.

Celia Maguire was the only person who still lived on an island when I was rowing up and down the lough. The other islands were home to wild birds and small animals, though sometimes I would moor my boat there too and talk with them. I'd stand in the ruins of an old monastery where monks had once prayed, or in the ruins of some abandoned cottage where quiet men in more recent times had listened to football matches on their wireless radio sets.

Not far from the shore at Aughakillymaude were the ruins of a house where two bachelors had once lived; two brothers who had loved each other magnificently. Even as children they had looked after each other. If one went fishing, the other would go along as well, just to keep an eye on him. If one was riding the big mare, the other would fuss along behind, telling him to go easy. When they were young men they had travelled to the mainland in search of women. But if one had an interest in a particular lady, the other would have just as equal a claim. In the latter end, neither of them married. They too remained on their island after their parents died, with a clean-scrubbed table and a fiddle hanging on the wall. And if the fiddle ever came down off the wall, the other would open a drawer and take out a flute and join in. The flute was coaxed into life, and it met the fiddle at a turn of a jig, and the two of them went off together in a hornpipe, as graceful as two horses trotting the road in step. People said they could play tunes like birds; in unison like the flight of geese. They were one at all times; the harmony between them was beyond human intelligence. Except for apples. One of them loved apples. The other couldn't keep an apple down.

One night, the apple lover was at home. And the other fellow was on the mainland. It was winter and there was ice

209

on the lough. In a deep sleep, the apple lover heard a voice. He woke. He could still hear it. In the frosty air, it travelled from the middle of the lake, from where his brother, the one who couldn't keep an apple down, was caught far out on the ice. He couldn't row to shore. He couldn't walk on the cold ice. So he called his brother. And his brother heard him. And his brother answered his call. Pulled out a boat from under the willows at the lough shore and pushed it out onto the ice. Took a pitchfork to break the frozen water. Made it deep into the white lake. Deep, but not deep enough, following the faint cries of his brother. The boy who could never keep an apple down. In the morning their boats were seen from the mainland, out in the middle of the lake. The two men were frozen to death. And the boats were so close together, their prows were touching.

It was getting dark as I got into the jeep and headed for home. At least I had a friend up there in the hills above Lough Allen. It was faint, but there was a sweet feeling of happiness in the twilight.

Of course there is nothing romantic about Mullingar. Donegal with its mountains and beaches is romantic. Mulraney Bay, Clare Island, the Cliffs of Moher or the shoreline of west Kerry are all romantic landscapes. And Leitrim, too, is on that list. The glens of north Leitrim are amazing. The Shannon runs through the county and the hills are wild and rugged with rush and heather, sheep and hawks. But Mullingar?

In 2006 I was happy to have left behind the constraints of marriage, but was left instantly broken-hearted and lonely without the love of my life. I had been melancholic for years, including all the years of my marriage. But I was still melancholic in Mullingar. Our moods follow us like a shadow. There is no escaping the interior weather. When I woke up alone and as free as any other single man in Mullingar, I didn't feel any happier. I lay there listening to the sound of glass being crushed in the breaker's yard down the street. It was rhythmic and monotonous; the crushing of windscreens, the exploding of whiskey bottles, the sweep of a million splinters, crush and sweep, crush and sweep, over and over again.

There was a notion in the nineteenth century that if you went away to the wilds, you could find your inner wildness. If you got to a space with no fences, then your mind would be without boundaries. Romantic poets could let loose their creativity, if they but owned a little cottage in some bee-loud glade in the country. And after a short time in a midlands town, I was beginning to miss the wilderness of the Leitrim hills very much. I was stuck in Mullingar with the breaking glass and the dog shitting from the grille of a third-floor balcony and the other dog shitting on the only little square of grass where children used to play in the summertime. By January 2007, after my first Christmas away from Leitrim, I realised that life wasn't going to be easy in Mullingar. My daughter had her schoolbooks, her Facebook and Bebo and her horses. I phoned the wife every evening and I'd tell her what I was cooking, but there was something missing. I was alone. Which is OK if you're twenty-five and have a future. But I was fifty-three. That's the bit I was missing.

So I ended up in bed, listening for the suck of the tide in the splintering glass, remembering the lions of my childhood who paced the cages of Dublin Zoo, watching a boy on the street who got a bike for Christmas spin in circles like a mad fly in a jam jar because he had nowhere to go.

Three years later, in 2010, I moved to Shandonagh House, a large old stone building on the edge of town, in the hope that I would be more content. One morning I looked out at tiny flecks of snow falling and a coy blackbird sitting on the trellis waiting for other birds and it thrilled me to be out of town at last, especially with the promise of snow in the sky.

A blue flame in the fire is the sign of a snowfall coming. But only if the flakes swarm like bees will it whiten the earth. I knew this snow would not last. There had been no blue flame in the fire the previous night. And these flakes did not swarm.

Sometimes I asked Polish friends, 'Is there anything you don't like about Ireland?'

They would say, 'You have only one season. You have no snow.'

I was ready for snow. I was standing there waiting for it to snow and thinking that it must be beautiful to be born in the snow or to make love in the snow or to die in the snow.

Years earlier, when I walked out on snowy mornings in the Leitrim hills, the silence made work impossible. Finishing the novel or clearing the drains or writing cheques or fretting in front of a computer screen about things as absurd as a career were not permissible when the soft snow fell to earth; enveloping the leafless naked bark of birch, weighing down the rusty beech leaf and the handle of a spade, covering and silencing everything.

Snow was a chance to check out of life; to abandon the empty self, to forget history, to leave aside every feud, wound, hurt or disgrace and begin again to play like a child and construct a new identity with frozen fingers in the big white wonder of a world made new. Snow meant time off to feed the birds and turn away. And as I stood at the door of my house in Mullingar, I was ready for snow.

214   I remember one time being at the bedside of an old man. The family members were in the kitchen praying. They thought he was dying. But he looked at me wickedly and offered me a cigarette. We smoked. It seemed strange that we would do something so mundane. He winked at me and said, 'I'm not ready to die yet.' And so he didn't. Not for another decade. We puffed our smoke and listened to the dirty rain splattering against the window and the galvanised roof.

'It's a dirty night,' he remarked.

He pointed towards the kitchen and said, 'There's a lock of neighbours down there in that kitchen, and they'll go before me.'

He was right. When he did die, it was snowing, and it covered the field where he fell, so that it was difficult to find him. And the neighbours brought him home to his house on the back of a door, and it was no exaggeration when his son said that he was frozen solid. I asked his wife what was he doing in the field on such a day.

'Nothing,' she said. 'He wasn't doing anything. He was just standing there.'

It was he who told me of the blue flame and the swarm of bees, as he smoked Sweet Afton in a cosy bed, ten years before that unmerciful snow folded him up in its blanket and took him away.

On the edge of winter in Shandonagh House one afternoon, I turned the radio off and stood at the back door, watching the flakes fall. I had three horses of clothes against the radiators; one in the kitchen, one in the hall and one in the bedroom. I had a lot of work to do. But I did nothing. I just stood there, waiting for snow. Hoping for snow. I was ready for snow.

And it did snow that winter, as I bunkered down in the big house surrounded by sycamore and chestnut trees just outside the town. It snowed for three weeks but I found no peace or consolation in it. Something in me hungered for a deeper wilderness.

In 1989 I spent the winter on a wild headland near Annagry in Donegal, just to watch the ocean beat off Tory in the moonlight. To listen in the morning to the waves of the sea break on the Trá Ban at Carraig na Finne.

And I remember hills around Lough Allen where I often walked a dog, hills which looked like Afghanistan on a wet day. The road curling up into the high ground beyond Arigna, where the wind screeched through empty mineshafts and over bare slag heaps, mounds of rock and shale and shifted earth, a graveyard of dead diggers and mining machinery. Bleak highways cut into the mountain to make a path for windmills, which had arrived years before, on lorries as big as any Yankie convoy in Kabul. The first time I heard the sound of a curlew, I thought it so forlorn that it sucked out all my neurosis and left me as clean as an empty bowl. Wilderness, I believed, was the mother of all poetry. I loved it. And I missed it.

216   After two years in Mullingar, I was prepared to travel 3,000 miles just to see birds nest on the edge of a cliff. I didn't know anything about birds, except that I used to love the cuckoo's call and the curlew's sean-nós song and the caw of sea gulls, laughing at the ocean. But I had been trying to finish the final draft of a show that became *The Tinker's Curse*, and I was tired. So the wild birds of Newfoundland seemed like the best reason to drop the work and to flee the streets of Mullingar for ten days. I got an invitation to perform a one-man show on St Patrick's Day. The show was called *Talking Through His Hat* in which I played Jonathan

Swift in an old coat that had once belonged to my Uncle Oliver and that the artist Heidi Wickham had transformed into a credible eighteenth-century jacket.

On my arrival in St John's, I was welcomed by members of the Irish community and I stayed in a timber house with bay windows. In the drawing room, there were old bookcases with leather-bound books, a silent harmonium and five white candles in a silver candelabra standing on the mantelpiece. The room was dominated by a grandfather clock that sliced the silence in even portions. I presented the show the following evening in a concert with the Irish piper Gabriel McKeon. Everything went well, the audience were delighted and delightful, and when it was over I danced with a woman I didn't know in a bar where Irish musicians were in session, and I kissed her outside on a street where the snow was packed into ridges seven-foot high.

Newfoundlanders throw great parties and they have beautiful eyes, a gift the sea bestows, and some faces are still haunted by shadows from far away and long ago. They are heroic, like birds blown off course in yesterday's storm. But they show none of this when they sing. When they sing, they fold themselves up in songs, and sing with the warmth of children at a log fire on Christmas Eve. The woman I kissed vanished into the snow but I stayed all night, listening to the singing, and at dawn one man discovered he had run out of matches for his cigarettes, so he went down the road and stood at the corner, flagging the morning traffic until he got lit up again. I looked out the window towards the harbour at a few rusting fishing boats and the lights of a cruiser just arrived from Philadelphia. Later I hired a car for a few days, drove down the coast and rented a cabin surrounded by birch trees on the southern shore. During the day, I walked along the cliffs and I dined each evening on salmon glazed with maple syrup at The Captain's Table.

At night, I lit a fire in the cabin and slept soundly in a big brass bed. In the middle of the night, I could hear the trees outside, whispering in the wind, just like they do in the hills above Lough Allen. I ate deep-fried cod, pan-fried cod, cod fillets, cod bake with cheese, chowder and even cods' tongues. Then I had more cod.

In the end I found the cliff I'd been looking for; the cliff at the end of the world, the cliff at the Cape where the gannets nest. Forty thousand of them. The onshore wind swept the stench of their droppings into my face, a whiff so fierce that it reminded me of the monkey house in Dublin Zoo. But they were beautiful, and I had found them; gannets stretching, kissing, preening, covering the sky above like confetti, diving into the ocean for fish, and then returning to the rock. And what troubled me was that even in that wild place each one of them seemed to have a companion. Kissing a strange woman had only reminded me of what I had missed since I'd left Leitrim. I had not expected that, and I felt overwhelmed with sorrow. I stood on the cliff's edge for a few moments and then I turned for home.

In the winter, we were devastated by funerals. On All Souls' Day we buried Frank McAuley, the squat man who had come in August and put in the stove. He'd had a sore throat in September and had gone for tests. They'd given him an all clear on the throat and he'd phoned Cathy to say how relieved he was. But a few days later, further tests had come back confirming that he had a number of advanced cancers in other places, and that his days were limited. His children had cried and his wife had cried and they had brought the bed downstairs and had made a bedroom out of the living room for the few weeks that remained.

Frank was a plumber. He was born of elderly parents on a small farm in 1942. There was no television or wireless in the cottage, and the roads and laneways about the house were silent and untarred. It rained for years as he grew up, and one day while he was picking potatoes with his father and his father was looking at the purple sky with great weariness, Frank decided that it was time to go away. So he found a job in a London factory and made friends with Cathy's two brothers, who took him under their wing, and brought him home to Portlaoise for holidays, where he happened to meet their teenage sister, who fell in love with him instantly and resolved to marry him.

He became a plumber and, a few years later, when the girl arrived in London, he danced with her in a sleeveless shirt and proposed marriage. Because of his trade, they were able to return to Ireland to rear their children.

Like plumbers all over the world, Frank knew an immense number of people in his locality and understood their worries and woes, because it is almost impossible not to confess your secrets to a man under the kitchen sink, or someone poking around in the hot press looking for a valve.

He loved his family and his pints, and he danced as straight as a rush with his wife, at weddings and christenings for many years. When the children had grown up and gone away to have more babies, he got a travel pass and before long there was no corner of Ireland that he had not seen.

We were delighted when he agreed to put in the stove for us. I was lying in bed exhausted, and envying him his good health as he drilled a big hole in the wall and stuck the pipe in and connected it to the back of the little black stove.

'I've never been a day sick in my life,' he'd said, 'thank God.'

And because he lived in the midlands, he'd been eager to sample the delights of a Leitrim pub at night. Being too sick, I hadn't been able to go with him but, in the morning, as he'd eaten a hearty breakfast, he'd told me of all the countrymen he'd met and the conversations he'd had.

A few weeks later, he'd gone to the doctor with a sore throat, and the doctor had sent him to a specialist. And when the specialist had said, 'Well it's not cancer,' he'd been shocked. He'd rung Cathy and said, 'I didn't even know they were looking for something as serious as that, but thank God they found nothing.' At least they found nothing in the throat.

That was in September. But, by the middle of October, tests had revealed cancer in other places, and when they took him into hospital one Friday night, he had barely enough breath to put his arm around his wife a few times and embrace all his children and grandchildren, before he was swept into a shadow.

In the open coffin in the front room of the house in Mountmellick where he'd lived, his face was white as marble. The corridor and hallway and rooms were full of neighbours in damp coats and black jackets, and the street outside was a sea of umbrellas, as the rain lashed down and the people recited a decade of the rosary. The priest waited at the gates of the cemetery the following day, the Feast of All Souls, while the sons carried their father shoulder-high. When he was put in the ground, one of them sang a folk song that was blown away in the wind. All around the graveyard, old emigrants chatted with old friends from the town. Eventually the crowd moved off towards the town, almost with an air of joy, refreshed and encouraged by the life of such a good man, and I returned to Leitrim and lit the stove and sat looking out at the lake for a very long time.

During November, I went a few times to my mother's house in Cavan, because it was empty. There was a statue of the Virgin with Child, a perfect blue and white example of that porcelain womanhood which withered when Germaine Greer wrote *The Female Eunuch*. The statue had stood on the bedroom mantelpiece until Mother had moved to a nursing home in Mullingar the previous year. I had tidied up the house the day she left and put the statue away in a box with holy pictures and other ornaments. But that November after Frank had been buried, I took the plaster Madonna out again and set her on a window ledge at the turn of the stairs, where she looked down on me as I ascended.

I thought motherly love might help me through the darkest days of winter. I hoped that the religious icon would console me. But it did not. It remained a chalky inanimate thing, and I sensed that my faith had finally dried up. Except for emails. In the weeks before Christmas I started sending emails out into the universe like prayers tossed into the grotto at Lourdes. Each day I sent messages to old friends, new friends and people who weren't really friends at all, but just happened to be in my contacts list. It was as if, in the dying days of the year, I had permission to say more than I normally said. I suppose people who are depressed sometimes find ways to unburden themselves.

'Sadness is not a bad thing,' I wrote to a friend, 'though lying in bed on a winter's day unable to do anything but weep is something most sensible people might try to avoid. Anyway, Happy Christmas.'

To an old girlfriend I wrote:

Hi there, hope you're well. Haven't been in contact for a long time. I suffered some ill health during the summer. So as I sit here by the stove I am thinking of you.

223

I still wonder what she thought of that, after thirty years. To another one I wrote a few pages, summing up the past few decades in my life, and then finished with the words:

But I am talking too much. It's more important to say I love you; you are a wonderful human being and that's all we need to know about the existence of God.

The emails were just a desperate attempt to sustain faith in something, during Ireland's twenty-first-century depression, as 70 per cent of the country worried about how to make ends meet in the coming year.

My mother didn't recognise us that Christmas; she was almost two years in the nursing home by then. We brought her a cardigan but she just looked at it and looked at me and said thank you, as she would to a stranger. And then just a few days after Christmas Cathy's brother Tom Byrne, who had sat on the patio in the rocking chair in August, finally gave up his battle with asbestosis and passed away.

Cathy and I flew to the funeral in London and Sophia came by boat and train, and had a rough crossing on a stormy winter sea. Tom had died in hospital with an oxygen mask, his children around him and his wife standing at the doorway, but I didn't think of him stretched on the cold slab of a hospital morgue. I thought of him as a boy, playing billiards in Thurles when he should have been doing his school homework. I imagined him on the boat for Holyhead, bristling with excitement, or outside a dancehall in drainpipe trousers or leaning over the wall on a summer's evening to chat with the sixteen-year-old English girl, Maureen, who became his lifelong companion.

The day after the funeral, a few of the family went to Brighton. I was in the front passenger seat. It was my first time in the town and though the wind was gale force, it wasn't cold. I was eating fish and chips outside Horatio's

Bar, sheltered from the storm by a glass wall, and from speakers above my head Bob Dylan bellowed out 'It Ain't Me Babe', a song I'd often sung as an adolescent, when I was frightened of intimate relationships and preferred exploring my own dark interior with narcissistic abandon.

A few guys in overcoats were collecting money from those going on the bumper cars. A gypsy woman with grey hair and a crystal ball wrapped an overcoat around her and sat in a barrel-top wagon waiting for customers – everything as it used to be in Bundoran in 1967. Except that I was on a long pier into the sea. Young couples laughed and clung to each other in the wind, but I remained in the shelter, for fear of losing my chips. I felt lost between sky and earth, comforted only by the sea around me, because water is attractive to people in sorrow, inviting them to dive right in and down and never come up again.

White horses heaved around the pier, the sand beneath making a muddy syrup of the sea. Birds rode the wind, waves crashed on the distant rocks and France was somewhere out there in the mist. Bob Dylan was still singing. The warrior. The one who endured. And I admired all that. Because the dead were dead and buried. And though I was almost sixty, the grim reaper had not yet called for me. And no matter how dark the day, it was incredibly wonderful just to be standing there, for a few moments, alone and alive on Brighton Pier.

I came home in early January and began again. I went

225

every day to the leisure centre, with renewed enthusiasm, and signed up for a course with a therapist in Dublin to talk out the knotted weave of all that hidden past which makes us human, and I knew that when I dived into the pool everything was OK. There was a shape to my body which found unity in the swim, and my mind, too, became coherent in the movement through water, in my goggle-eyed observation of the blue floor and the occasional shiny black of another swimmer's costume.

In that chlorinated world, I could hear the gurgling of everything that had ever happened in my life, from my first womb waking to the previous night's dreams. And I knew that if I kept swimming and listening in that silent underwater refuge, then everything that should arise would arise. Whatever hidden hurt or wound there may have been in childhood, when anxiety had grown like mushrooms on the wall of an unopened room, it would all emerge and come to the surface of consciousness eventually, as I swam my way into the future. That, I suppose, was my hope for the new year.

Part Three

Swallowing the clouds

As my recovery gathered momentum in the spring of 2012, I tried to get back to work. The idea of performing on stage seemed, as yet, too stressful, so I looked about for work on movies. In June, I got a part in a film being shot in Ireland called *Run and Jump* in which I played a character who dies suddenly.

I stayed in the Wilton Hotel in Bray the night before the shoot, and was brought to the set near Roundwood at 6.40 a.m. in a big black Mercedes. I got costumed in a black suit and tie and the make-up department transformed my hands into white marble claws and my face into the pallid lifeless mask of the dead. I walked from there to the house where the shooting was to take place, and felt a chill as the crew looked on. 'Dead man walking,' a member of the crew cried out as a joke, but nobody laughed.

It was an ordinary modern house, in its own grounds. Big and cosy with timber floors in the hallway, soft sofas in the study and a stove fire in the drawing room. Lots of mourners were standing around taking tea and eating sandwiches, and a dark oak coffin was situated on a plinth in the front room. It was a normal wake, except that the corpse was not yet in the coffin and everyone was looking at me.

The fact that there were electricians and sound technicians and assistant directors on the edges of the activity didn't matter. The fact that there was a young man from Alabama behind the lens of a large camera at the far end of the room or that there were spotlights on stands in the corners didn't matter either. The only thing that concerned me was that, for the next few hours, I was going to be dead. I was gone from the world. And the people in the room were staring at me as if I was already decaying. I would have no part in the forthcoming activities. I was required to do nothing except be dead.

The coffin was the main attraction and it was time to get in. Nobody around me knew that I had been through a year of depression. Nobody knew the grief that illness had awakened in my soul. And this was only a movie. But even as such, the room was full of real people, and for the sake of a movie we were all expected to act out a ritual. And in that ritual, I was dead. I could feel the isolation. I alone was required to lie helpless and motionless in the coffin.

The coffin was laced inside with the usual blue trimmings. I climbed in and lay flat, my head on a small pillow. The costume department fixed the lace again around my head and body so that my face and hands were exposed. I noticed immediately that coffins are narrow. There's no space for elbows, since of course dead people don't need any elbowroom. The costume department shoved my elbows down so that my two white dead marble hands stuck up. They entwined my fingers, and then laced a rosary beads around the fingers. And that was it. For about three hours.

Coffins are not cushioned inside, since the dead don't feel any tiredness in their backs, but, after an hour, I began to experience severe pain. People came up to the coffin, and looked in, and cried, and held each other, and comforted each other, and one or two touched my fingers or made the sign of the cross on my forehead with their thumb. I longed for one of the mourners to kiss me. To press their lips on my forehead. But nobody did. I was untouchable. A child entered the room and her mother said, 'Go over and look at the corpse,' but the child said, 'No, I don't want to, I'm afraid,' and she fled the room.

I could almost smell decay as one does in a stuffy room

231

where a corpse is laid out. In the texture of blue lace around my face and body, I could feel death and smell decay. And I knew that these hours in the coffin were like a rehearsal for some later time, when my body will be returned to a coffin and left in it forever. The coffin is a cradle of death that waits for everyone and I knew that from that day forward I could never again touch my beloved's body, or look at the flowers of spring or rejoice in the moon reflecting on a lake without also knowing that this would be the end of the journey.

And I realised that the unbearable grief of that knowing is what I had carried like a lump in my throat and a stone in my heart all my life. Knowing that it ends is an instinct within us all. That life fails even though we try so hard to succeed. We try to work at jobs or careers, or develop hobbies or adventures that will assure us of some sense of success. Most of all we try to make love succeed. We store up illusions about sex companionship or children being a ground of being that lasts forever, when, in truth, the libido fades and even couples grow apart and children, of necessity, must turn their back on the old in order to claim the future.

The grief of being mortal is the stain in the heart that colours all our unconscious activity, and only when that grief surfaces can we wake to the real beauty of life, which exists in the moment and is therefore transient.

I suppose it was a lot to be thinking about in the coffin,

but it passed the time while the director got her film into the can, and I held my breath a few times when she wanted close-ups of my dead face. And then I went back to the hotel a changed man.

I can see now why mediaeval saints sometimes slept in their own coffins, why Buddhist monks loiter in graveyards and why shamanist therapists in the West train themselves by digging their own graves and staying overnight underground.

Later that evening, I had won ton soup with sweet and sour chicken delivered to the hotel bedroom by the local Chinese takeaway. I watched the news and rejoiced in being alive for a few more hours or days or years, and in the morning I went to see my therapist.

Won ton soup contains delicate dumplings, spiced meat or vegetables wrapped in pastry. The dumplings always remind me of the more bulky momo, a heavier dumpling served in a meat broth in Tibet and Mongolia. Won ton means to swallow the clouds, and the dumplings do resemble clouds, if you use your imagination a little. But the momos are more substantial and I became a fan of them in Mongolia in the summer of 1999. It was the only occasion in my life when I took an opportunity to leave home and go to the ends of the earth in order to find peace. It was at the peak of my engagement with Buddhist practice and I thought that if I made a great journey, a pilgrimage, even in middle age, I might find some peace of mind. And I did. I found it, but not exactly in the way that I had expected.

The most beautiful lake I ever saw was in Mongolia. It was called Khovsgol. It was two hundred and fifty metres deep and it was over one hundred and twenty kilometres long. I was told that it was the clearest lake in the world, and the coldest. It was called 'the dark-blue pearl of Mongolia', and it was certainly dark blue and beautiful when I stood on its shoreline one summer long ago, when the mountain peaks surrounding it had still been covered with snow, even though it was summertime. And of all the lakes in the world that I have ever seen, Khovsgol was the most wonderful and haunting.

I went there with an old Tibetan monk and a nurse from Switzerland called Heidi. For me, the entire thing started out as an accident. The monk, who lived in west Cavan, was going on a mission and he needed someone to accompany him and I was asked if I would like to assist. And I said yes. It was as simple as that. At first, I had no real purpose in going. It just seemed like a good idea to tag along with the lama. My passport and flights were all arranged with his by the staff at the Buddhist centre. I didn't have to do anything, until I found myself one evening in his bedroom in Jampa Ling as he tried to pack his suitcase. Margery, the director of the centre, was there as well. We both sat on the bed watching him. I hadn't seen a Tibetan monk pack a suitcase before and I haven't seen the operation since, but once in a lifetime might be enough. The case was filled and closed and then something that had been forgotten was remembered and the case was opened and emptied and packed again and closed again and then something further was mentioned that had been forgotten. And the process was repeated. It went on for most of the evening until I was exhausted just watching him, and I slipped off down the corridor to get a night's sleep.

The following morning, Margery drove both of us to Belfast and the monk and I left on a British Midlands flight for London and met up with Heidi at Heathrow. She had short blonde hair like a boy and was wearing a yellow anorak. Together we boarded an Aeroflot flight for Moscow. On the plane, there was a group of young Russian girls with bare arms and long necks and white lace blouses and ponytails and I lusted for them from a safe distance two rows behind. *Perhaps they are ballet dancers*, I thought, because they strode to the bathroom every so often with such elegance.

We just wanted a connecting flight to Mongolia, but the planes had been delayed and the next flight was not until the following day. And we didn't have visas for Russia. Since we had intended travelling directly on to Mongolia, we didn't think we needed them. But this displeased the

236

lady at check-in who was dealing with us. She explained that without visas we could not move around the airport.

The monk in maroon robes and black-rimmed glasses looked exhausted, and he limped because his knee had been smashed years earlier. Heidi, an air steward with Swissair, who also worked as a nurse in a hospice for the dying in Zurich, could do nothing, so she went off somewhere and returned with three ice-cream cones. She was in her early thirties and had blue eyes and beautiful white teeth. She smiled at the woman behind the check-in desk and asked her if she wanted an ice-cream. The Russian lady said no. We ate our ice-creams and just stood, like geese who'd landed on the wrong shore, until a bad-tempered, overweight man in a loose grey suit and sweating like a pig brought us to a minibus outside. Then we were whisked away to a hotel, where we were imprisoned on the second floor until it was time for our flight the following evening.

After twenty-four hours in Moscow under close surveillance, we were taken back to the airport and put on a flight for Ulaanbaatar, which took eight hours. The plane was narrow and the seats were tiny and a woman beside me offered me boiled sweets. She was huge. I was squashed in between her and the window and she kept practising her English on me all the way across the world.

'I am Mongolian woman,' she said. 'I have job in Moscow. I go home now to Mongolia. I live Ulaanbaatar. Would you like another sweet? Would we like another sweet? Ha ha.

Would they like another sweet? Would I ask the pilot if he wants sweet? Ha ha.'

The monk was stretched across three empty seats behind me, sleeping as soundly as a baby. But sometimes I felt he was watching me and sometimes I thought he was laughing inside.

'Would you like another sweet?'

'No, thank you.'

And after eight hours, the plane began gliding down silently into a land of silence, and we arrived in Ulaanbaatar.

We processed through passport control in orderly fashion. Heidi smiled at me. And I smiled back. Mothers and children stared at us. Brothers and cousins embraced, and moved from foot to foot, edgy with excitement, and eager to get round the corner and into the public lobby.

We were edging forward. Heidi and I pushed the two luggage trolleys and flanked the tiny monk in his maroon robes. Beyond passport control, we rounded a corner and everything changed. There were hundreds of people crowded into the main foyer of the airport, beyond the steel barriers that protected the arrivals as they came through from the luggage carousel. And the crowd erupted into applause when they saw the monk. People fussed and squashed together and pressed forward, and monks held the line by joining hands, holding everyone back, allowing us to pass through the sea of people to the kerb outside where there was a white Mercedes and a blue Toyota jeep,

238

with blue silk scarves tied to the bonnets and to the radio aerials, idling in the morning sun.

The monk was put into the Mercedes, and a swell of monks milled behind him and surrounded the car and squashed their faces to the windows to see him. The crowd remained silent, but swayed and heaved towards the door in a collective effort to be near him. A young man with hooded eyes held my elbow firmly and directed me to the back of the Mercedes. I thought he was a policeman or a security guard. But then I noticed he, too, was wearing robes.

'Welcome to Mongolia,' he said. 'We met in India. I cooked your noodles.'

The Mercedes and the jeep drove into the centre of Ulaanbaatar, where there was a welcoming ceremony at the gates of the Lamrim Monastery. People processed from the street in through the gates and up the steps of the Prayer Hall. After them, the monks lined up and chanted as they walked in, and behind them came the frail old monk we had accompanied from Ireland. They called him the Rinpoche, and clearly he was a very important figure in Mongolia. Monks wore bright red cloaks and yellow hats that looked like gigantic slices of lemon. Women wore blue silk dressing gowns and most of the men were in denim jeans and white shirts with white peaked caps like golfers in America. Some people were squashed against the sides of an old blue truck in the corner of the monastery grounds.

239

Then some men got up on the back of the truck and someone opened the door so that five or six young children could get inside. They had a great view from there of the procession of lemon heads as they chanted and processed into the hall. When the Prayer Hall was full to the doors, the rest straggled up the steps and filled the veranda. Drums battered. Long silver horns called out like elephants.

The Prayer Hall was dark inside and the Rinpoche mounted a throne in front of the shrine. He had to climb up four wooden steps painted red and it was clear that his sore leg was making it difficult. Other monks rushed to manoeuvre him, step by step, to the red-cushioned throne where he sat in the lotus position and looked utterly exhausted. The abbot, an old bald man with a wiry body and cunning face, spoke a formal welcome to the Rinpoche from Ireland, and a tall stick of a monk with saintly blue eyes translated into Tibetan so that the Rinpoche could understand. The monk with the hooded eyes who had cooked for me in India five years earlier stood beside the throne, sorting out blue scarves on his arm, taking them from his shoulder bag and laying them out over his forearm.

The old monks sat close to the Rinpoche, while the young ones were farther away. All sat in the lotus position with a simple red wooden bench in front of each person for their prayer book or their soup bowl. There was a centre aisle, and two side aisles not occupied by monks. This space was now flooded with people from the street until they were jammed like sardines in a tin.

Heidi had moved in among them, her eyes on the Rinpoche, and she struggled in the crowd to get as close as she could to him. I was at the back door, mildly offended by the smell. The butter lamps threw out a distinct aroma. And the poor unwashed people sweated in old clothes and gave off a powerful hum. And there was a well-used toilet close by. And the monks discharged an intolerable amount of incense on top of everything else. Great funnels of incense spiralled up and twisted into a blue cloud above the people. And it was stuffy. There was no ventilation and little oxygen, and the doors had been closed all morning, and the monks had been sitting for hours, waiting for the Rinpoche, praying and belching and farting.

The people made a procession like a snake in a clockwise direction around the walls of the Prayer Hall and when each one came close to the throne, the young monk from India, Losang Rabsal, flicked a blue scarf into their hands. Each one then approached the Rinpoche with a blue scarf hanging over joined hands and with bowed heads. The Rinpoche took each scarf, blessed it and returned it, placing it around the shoulders of the same person. The procession continued until all the people had bowed and touched the Rinpoche and everyone in the hall was decked with a blue scarf, including Heidi. Everyone except for me. I was still at the door, still inundated with this sudden swell of human devotion. For a moment, everyone was silent and still and then suddenly a giant drum cried out and a cymbal clashed and the monks began again a low drone from the pit of their bellies and their sung prayers filled the darkness and mingled with the smell of the butter candles and the farts of the monks.

When the ceremony of welcome was over, the Rinpoche, Heidi and the entourage who had collected him from the airport went off to an apartment somewhere in Ulaanbaatar. I didn't know what lay ahead of me, or what was required of me, but I was given a small room in the monastery and told to stay there. It was a monk's cell, containing a box-shaped bed and a shelf on which the monk had set a figure of a Buddha and some candles. The toilet was next door; a well-used hole in the ground stinking to high heaven.

Heidi was higher in the pecking order than me, and since we had landed she had become my link with the Rinpoche and his entourage. Before they had all left, she'd explained that I must remain in the monastery on my own for a few days until everything was organised. She'd said that the Rinpoche intended to make a journey into the north-west of the country. He was looking for the site of a monastery, she'd said, where he wanted to ordain some young men. During the time of the Soviets, a lot of monasteries in Mongolia were destroyed and the monks were sent to prison camps. Their memory was erased and their names airbrushed from the maps. But now the maps were being remade. Old sites were being rediscovered. Ancient centres of learning were rising again out of the ground. The Rinpoche's trip, Heidi had explained, was part of a greater strategy on behalf of Tibetan Buddhists to assist in the reconstruction of the monastic tradition in Mongolia.

'And why did you come?' she'd wondered.

'I don't know,' I'd replied.

I was exhausted from the travel and almost glad to see them go as I waved at the Mercedes and the jeep. But what really surprised me was that all the other monks in the monastery went home as well. In accordance with the restrictions imposed by the Soviet system, celibacy was not encouraged and so most monks were married. So at 5 p.m. every evening, they all went home. It was a strange sight, a sort of monastic rush hour as they headed off to their wives and children. And I was left behind. In my room. The doors were locked and, though I could walk about the corridors inside or visit the Prayer Hall, I was in fact a prisoner. I looked from the small window in my room and saw that the gates were also locked. I was a prisoner in a mediaeval building. And this, according to Heidi, would be the situation until we were ready for the journey because the apartment they had rented had no space for me.

They left me a pot of dumplings and a bucket of horse's milk with a ladle and two bowls in case I needed food in the night. Heidi had warned me about the milk. She said it was ceremonial. She said that whenever we went into the

243

country and met people in their tents, they would give us bowls of mare's milk. And it was important to drink it. But she admitted that in all the months she had been travelling with the Rinpoche, she had never been able to stomach it.

I decided there was only one way to condition myself to the milk, since I had a bucket of it under the bed and nothing to do for the rest of the evening but wander around the prayer halls and look at the garish Buddhas in the flickering light of butter candles that were still burning on various shrines. And if I dealt with the milk now, I would be able to impress Heidi when we went on the road and show her that I was an intrepid traveller.

So I ladled out a bowl of milk and began drinking. Unfermented mare's milk can be a strong laxative, and can create intestinal difficulties. But I took my chances. It had a pungent smell, it was pungent on the tongue and left an aftertaste of almonds. Almost immediately I wanted to urinate.

But I succeeded in drinking an entire bowl. Then I thought that one more bowl would do the trick. So I ladled out another slop of it, up to the brim, and began again with my two hands to sup. And before I was halfway through, it had indeed done the trick. I had overcome any revulsion and was beginning to enjoy it. By the time I took my third bowl an hour later, I thought the stuff as smooth and pleasing as a pint of Guinness.

Being locked in excited me. Heidi excited me. The

butter lamps and the flickering garish images of Buddhas excited me. I undressed and lay down and tried to sleep even though it was only about eight o'clock. I stripped down to a vest and lay on top of the open sleeping bag because it was warm. I dozed for a short while and then woke suddenly with an erection. I was hot and distended and rock hard, and my cock felt like the core of my being. As if the rest of my body was a small appendage connected to a floating phallus. It seemed funny at first but, as time went by, I became alarmed at the intensity of the condition. It surpassed anything I had ever enjoyed on the wildest nights of boyhood. It was a sudden and powerful muscular sensation which flowed out from the cock and moved through my belly and thighs. I felt inward convulsions at the core that were then surfacing on my skin. And they were growing ever stronger and stronger, and they brought me beyond any experience of sexual arousal I'd ever had in my life. And yet there seemed no object for this condition. And no end in sight, and so intensely did I feel my mind dissolving into erotic sensation that I became frightened. My body was turning into an enormous penis and not a woman in sight. Not a human in sight. I was a phallus, enclosed in a monastery. Maybe it was jet lag. Maybe the Mongolian woman on the plane with the sweets spiked my orange juice. Maybe it was the aroma of candles and the horse's milk.

I lay flat on the bed for a long time, hard and warm,

245

sweating and frightened, and eventually I began to allow my imagination to dwell on female Buddha images coupling with their consorts on the walls around me. I could have brought images of my beloved to mind. I could have recalled images of film stars. But it would have seemed a sacrilege to induce fantasies of a human nature in this mediaeval monastery. So I stuck with the female Buddhas. Even when the room filled with darkness, I remained hot and sweaty and I longed for a shower, but instead I lay without moving until I fell asleep. In the morning I felt refreshed, and I hadn't the slightest sign of a hangover.

R absal, the monk with the hooded eyes, came to me every day with buckets of dumplings and rice and bottles of orange and buckets of horse's milk. He told me not to leave the monastery on my own, but sometimes we walked together up the road, between the huckster shops, and through the shantytown and past other monasteries.

One day, he spoke to me about his mother. When he was finished, I felt an urge to phone my own mother to tell her that I loved her. But there were no phones. So, instead,

I told Rabsal that I'd like to go to the post office and send some postcards.

It was Wednesday afternoon and it was hot in Ulaanbaatar. The streets were dry and dusty and little children in bare feet followed us all the way. At one point, Rabsal bought them doughnuts and took their photographs.

There was a rack of postcards on sale inside the door of the post office. Pictures of Yaks. Mongolians in traditional hats, sitting on horses. Archers. Wrestlers. Images of Buddha or Genghis Khan. I sent postcards to Dublin, Cork, Belfast, Cavan and Bawnboy. To my mother I wrote:

Hi Mam – here among the Yaks. Having a great time. Love you very much.

I felt better after that. But it was even hotter as we walked back. And we had to watch the dusty tracks in the shantytown because the ground was covered with dog poo and we were in sandals. And there were lots of dogs in the shantytown. Wolf-like creatures with amber eyes, stalking strangers. And huckster shops on the corners. Little galvanised huts selling religious trinkets, which reminded me of the Marian Shrine in Knock in the summers of my childhood.

'Where are we going now?' I asked, when I realised that Rabsal was not heading back directly to the monastery.

'To a hospital,' he said. 'New hospital!'

In fact, he brought me to a building site; an empty shell without water, sanitation or toilet plumbing, and, of course, no patients. In its cavernous interior, we roamed for half an hour, with cement dust in our noses, looking for 'the French woman'. She was tall and grey-haired, and spoke with ferocious zeal about her intentions regarding maternity units, showers, baths and toilets. 'And all will be free,' she declared, 'for the poor.'

Then after spending as long as one can staring at a building site, I asked Rabsal what should we do next.

'Post office,' he said.

'But we've been there,' I said.

'No,' he said, 'we must make phone call.'

So off we went in the heat, back to the post office which was a mile away. Making a phone call was far more complicated than just posting a letter. Inside the post office, there were rows of telephone kiosks. First we checked in at reception and took a form. The form required us to fill in a name, address and the phone number that we wanted to call. This Rabsal did and handed it in at another glass window. From here we were directed upstairs to kiosk number twenty-five. So up we went and waited for the phone to ring.

Rabsal was phoning his niece in Moscow. When the phone rang, he lifted the receiver but all he could hear was an engaged tone. So we tried again, going through

249

all the same rituals. We tried four times. An hour had passed.

'Maybe phone number wrong! What to do now?' he said, looking terribly disappointed.

I watched him for a while as he stood still, and his logic seemed to be that since we had come to make a phone call, we should not be deterred because this particular number didn't answer.

'I make call to Beijing instead,' he suggested. So we rang a Beijing number. There was no reason to call. And we got through to an old woman who was mystified as to why we were calling her from Mongolia. And because she spoke English better than Rabsal spoke Chinese, I was put on to talk with her. I explained that I was Irish and that I was standing beside a Mongolian who was a friend of her son. But neither of us actually knew her. She said it was raining in Beijing and that opened up possibilities. We talked about the weather for a long while. Then I whispered to the now gleeful Rabsal beside me.

'What else will I say? Tell me quick! Why am I calling?'

The woman in China also wanted to know why we were calling.

Rabsal seemed perplexed. 'Oh yes,' he exclaimed, 'you thank her for the milk!'

And so I thanked her for the dried milk her son had sent the previous winter when it was very cold. And that completed our mission. And that was Wednesday. We had planned a phone call. And we had made a phone call. The day had been a success.

Rabsal walked me home and left me in the monastery and I saw him go out the gate and down the road to wherever he was staying. Because he was not staying with the Rinpoche and I did not know from whence he came each day or to where he went each evening when he bade me farewell. He came back the following day as usual with more dumplings and milk and stories of his childhood and after a week I imagined that I knew him very well.

Rabsal was born from the womb of a beautiful young woman in a tent covered with snow. He was that mother's only child, though there were cousins his own age in nearby tents. It was a huge family of many people, in many tents, surrounded by an abundance of sheep.

His father was old. He was small and thin and unpleasant. Like a snake standing erect, with huge ears, and in his throat a constant whistle of wind. In those days, all the young children would eat dried fruit, which they called 'old people's ears'. Rabsal called them 'father's ears'.

His father was a threat. A dangerous being. A little emperor on the hills, with his two tents and his few hundred animals. He sat on the grass in summer, motionless, like a log of wood in the forest. A felled tree. There was always something hurt in him that was not spoken. If you went close, you could feel the anger of his still body, like the heat of a fire. He wore a peaked cap. Black and greasy. Beneath

251

it, his face was a little coconut with wisps of beard under his chin. A cigarette always in his mouth. He passed his days watching people. As sly as an unwanted cat.

In my imagination, Tibet was wandering around in tents. Following animals. Playing with bells. Stirring soup. Smoking pipes. The coldest part of the night was just after dark until bedtime. Rabsal's young cheeks burned with the cold air. And he sat in the corner of the tent dreaming of monasteries. He did not desire cattle. He did not desire horses. He did not desire yaks. He did not desire a wife or child or to be beautiful and be praised by the village. All these he controlled with the lash of the cold wind. The only thing he desired was a monastery. And that, he thought, was a proper desire. A noble desire. It was a desire that would make him strong. And make his mother proud.

How wonderful to be inside the walls of a monastery. Learning to read. With a warm stove and an old Mongolian teacher to shorten the evenings. With stories like 'The Empty Pot' and 'The Upside Down Pot' and 'The Pot with the Hole in the Bottom'.

At night, he would sometimes stand out with the horses. The horses kicked the wind. They were angry with the cold air.

Rabsal spoke to them. 'Don't be disappointed with the cold wind. I am also disappointed. You want shelter. But I, Rabsal, wish for a monastery. We are not so different.'

He rubbed one horse's nose, and stared into its eyes until the horse settled.

'I am Buddha,' he whispered, and the horse whinnied with fright, and Rabsal fell into the snow laughing.

The old man was turning into air. A shadow in the corner. Always in the dark of the tent now. Even through the hot summer. On the bed. Yellow in the face. A putrid smell from his piss. He was in pain when he moved. His legs swelled with sores. And his tooth ached in the middle of the night.

One day he turned to his son and said, 'You were born stupid. You will never get a wife.'

'I don't want a wife,' Rabsal said. 'I want to go to the monastery.'

The old man laughed till it hurt his ribs and he coughed black phlegm up as his laughter turned to choking. The following day, he was dead. His body was washed and taken away for a sky burial. Up the hill to be chopped to pieces and fed to the vultures. Rabsal did not cry. Soon after they had taken the body away, he went out with a bucket to fill it with snow for the cooking. When he was there in the open space, the white light of the snow filled his head and for the first time he realised his father was gone. It felt as if the world was beautiful and empty, and it made him dizzy.

He brought the snow bucket into the tent and placed it over the stove and made a brew of good tea with butter for his mother, who sat in the corner, fingering her beads.

253

When the tea was ready, he took a surprise out of his pocket and wrapped it in a white scarf and handed it to her with both hands outstretched, and his body bent low before her. His mother opened the scarf slowly, and discovered two little plastic Buddhas, each one no bigger than the top of her thumb. She lifted them, as if she were taking eggs from a nest, and looked lovingly at her son. The darkness had gone from their tent.

'Where did you get them?' she asked. But he never told her.

By springtime of the following year, the smell of stale piss was completely gone. The fragrance of jasmine, milk and butter filled the tent. His mother would unwind her long hair from her headscarf and gaze at him through the shafts of sunlight that flooded down through the gap in the roof. Summer was like that. The animals minded themselves. And she did, indeed, loosen her skirts and ache with joy.

254

But Rabsal was unprepared for the cause of his mother's bliss. Another man had come. A man with a moustache and a gap between his front teeth. He patted Rabsal on the head. They said that, at first, he had come to mind the animals. But he ended up minding everyone. His name was Sera. That winter, he minded Rabsal's mother. Wanu, he called her. Rabsal had never heard her called that before. Wanu. The first thing Rabsal saw each morning in the tent was Sera, wiry and watchful, standing over the stove with bread in his hand. The emptiness of the world had not lasted long.

But one day Wanu and Sera had a row. It was just before Sera headed off on one of his journeys. Each month, he made a journey to the town. He would be gone for four or five days.

'I would need to be a magician,' Sera was complaining, 'to remember all you tell me.'

'Then write it down,' Wanu said. 'This is the modern age. We can hear things on the radio now. We must live like other people.'

'But your lists are endless,' he said, waving the paper in her face. 'Look, powders and creams. That's all this is. There are more important things for me to remember.'

He rushed through the door of the tent in his long coat. She went after him. Rabsal watched as they argued across the back of the pack mule. Then they made up. She could tell, because Wanu was buttoning up Sera's coat to the chin. And she was rubbing the back of her hand on his frozen moustache to take the snow away. And then Sera squeezed her. Wanu was slight and delicate, like a flower, and the big hero in his coat was winding his arms around her and lifting her off her feet.

They both returned to the tent. Wanu was crying. Sera was crying. They sat down and after a while he took off his coat and Wanu poured him a bowl of soup and then she said, 'It is late. You must wait until tomorrow.'

All evening, there was peace and silence in the tent, and Rabsal was drawn into it. The two grown-ups made love under the blankets, and Rabsal closed his eyes and dreamed of a monastery where big birds hung from hooks on the wall, ready for the cooking pot. He dreamed of kitchen tables laden with vegetables and prayer halls of polished bowls, and silver candle-holders and silk prayer flags and giant thangkas – Tibetan silk paintings – hanging from the roof and drums and pipes and cushions and stoves and old monks and bottles of snuff and shelves of hats and corridors of voices.

The bodies beneath the blanket lay still. Sera ladled himself another bowl of soup and Wanu raddled the fire and placed dried dung on the hot ash to redden the stove once more.

'I couldn't bear prison,' Sera whispered. 'I would go mad.'

The fire was blazing. Rabsal was pretending to sleep. But he heard it all. 'I couldn't bear prison.' They were staring into the fire. They were frightened.

Outside a dog began to bark. They all listened. His mother got up and made herself ready to sleep on her own couch. Sera stayed at the fire. His back against a bed box. His eyes open and focused on some distant world. The dog barked through the night. The snow whispered on the tent. Every time Rabsal turned, he woke. And every time he woke, he saw the steady hawk eyes of Sera, gazing into the fire. In the morning, the fire was blazing. The stove was red hot. And no one asked about the dog. Rabsal and his mother had sleep in their eyes and in their mouths. They wrapped themselves in blankets and savoured the hot tea that Sera had made. The tea washed away their dreams, as they sat at the warm, blazing fire he had kept on all night.

Sera belted his coat in the tent and covered his face with a scarf. He pulled the fur hat down over his ears and onto his eyebrows. Rabsal was a happy cat by the fire; the pleasure of remaining when someone else is leaving. Sera left without a word.

When he was gone, they sat listening to the horse's protest. The muffled sound of hooves in the snow for a few seconds. But before he was twenty metres away from them, there was complete silence. The few days that followed were calm. So white and still and so gentle that Rabsal and his mother walked around without anxiety, following their routines, as if in a dream.

257

Rabsal was hiding in the interior compartment of a bed box when the soldiers arrived. His mother had squeezed him into it at the very last moment. But the soldiers went directly to the bed. Pulled away the blankets. Lifted the lid. And dragged the frightened child up into the air, with a sweep of one arm. His mother was screaming.

'Don't hurt my child.'

The soldiers were saying Sera's name. Shouting it. Slapping Rabsal in the face.

'You know him. He has been here. Where did he go?'

Rabsal fell to the floor. His mother continued to scream. The soldiers lifted him by the hair again. Shook him by the shoulders. Slapped him again about the face.

'Your mother is a slut,' they shouted. 'She hides criminals under her skirts. You must tell us the truth or else you will turn out like her. She will tell us only lies, but you must tell us the truth.'

Then they left. It was quiet for another few days. The mornings were full of snow and cloud, and it was difficult to get out of bed. In the afternoons, it brightened. The sky was open, endless and blue. Everything was still and hidden in the fresh white falling.

'I won't let them do that to you again,' Wanu said. She was cracking ice in a bucket.

'But next time we must find you a better hiding place.'

One night, before she went to sleep, Wanu took her son's thumb, placed it in her mouth and sucked it. The child stood watching her sucking it. Feeling her love in every movement of her lips. As if she was telling him something. As if her body and tongue were imparting all the wisdom and fire of her mind into that little thumb.

The snow was blue. The days continued to turn. Ice rain fell on the tent during the night when the fire was low, making it heavy in the mornings, and cooling everything inside. The cold would waken them, and they would lie together. But each day was getting colder. His mother said that she knew an uncle of hers who went out one day in weather like that without wearing a hat to cover his ears. After a few minutes, he felt pain in his ear. He banged it with his fist, thinking to warm it, but his hand passed his head and his ear fell to the ground.

'That's how cold it is outside now,' Wanu told him. They huddled closer. And his mother's hair fell on either side of her face as she slept on the pillow beside him.

'Like a wishing jewel,' Rabsal whispered. 'Like some precious thing,' he told me, 'my mother was going into my thumb.'

Every day, Wanu would touch it. Hold it between her fingers. Squeeze it between her teeth. And the frost made the tent as stiff as the bark of a tree. Her mother opened the document box belonging to her husband. In it was a transistor radio set. They fiddled with it until they got the BBC World Service. They would sit down each day and listen to the world news, and the news about Britain. They were able to say the words.

First Wanu would say, 'The World News!'

And Rabsal would say, 'This is London!'

As if it were a form of greeting. Neither of them understood a word of English, but it was something to hope in. It, too, was a wishing jewel.

The day the soldiers returned, Rabsal was sitting in the pen by the stove with a sheep that suffered from blindness because of the snow. Three soldiers entered the tent. An old

259

one with greasy hair and two teenage boys. The boys were too small for their uniforms, but they both had guns over their shoulders. They dragged Wanu outside. They didn't even notice the boy in the box with the sheep.

He heard Wanu screaming. He heard the sound of his mother being beaten with long sticks. Then he peeped out through a slit in the door of the tent. The young soldiers were strapping a rope to the crossbeam of the hut where the animals sheltered. They were going to hang her.

The older soldier was sitting at the door of the jeep talking to his driver, another old man. They paid little attention to the fury of the two teenagers. In the struggle to expose the woman's neck they tore her shirt so that her breasts were exposed, which upset Rabsal because it was very cold. He did not think of his mother being hanged. He thought only that her breasts were being exposed to the cold air.

260   They tied her wrists behind her back and then tied her feet together at the ankles. Noosed her neck and pulled the rope. She flew up a foot, and dangled and struggled and her mouth was blue. They jolted the rope again. Higher. Then down. And she fell like a sack of grain onto the snow. But Rabsal saw her eyes open again. As if they were about to pop out. Big white bulging marbles as she lay in the snow. Then the older man at the jeep shouted something at the teenagers. The boys stopped and returned to the jeep, muttering to themselves and grumbling that they hadn't

been allowed finish their job. Rabsal was thinking, *She will recover. She will be well. Perhaps her neck is damaged. But I will make ointment for the burns and she can lie flat for as long as it takes for the soreness to go. I will cook and make fires. It will be well.*

Then he saw the older soldier walk over to where his mother lay and put his pistol to her chest and shoot into her five or six times. The soldier tossed the cigarette he was smoking onto the snow, and Rabsal could hear it sizzle and die, and he heard the jeep cough into life and the soldiers arguing with each other over the noise of the engine as they drove away. His mother's blood moved like a snake from her tattered breasts, in a meandering line in the snow, and then it stopped. The blood was absorbed by the snow, making the snow crimson, and Rabsal covered her breasts with his coat.

There were days when I asked myself why I was stuck in a monastery in Mongolia, and the only answer I could come up with was that I had been infatuated by the Rinpoche. There is something about a father figure that I could never resist; from the memory of my own father's deathbed to the face of Pope John Paul II, the ghost of fatherhood has always mesmerised me. And so here I was, obedient and loyal to another human being who came from a world I did not know or understand, and whose mind was as remote from me as the mind of God.

Or perhaps in such old men I have gathered and stored the fragments of what once was a god. What was once coherent love in all its powerful mythic manifestation. I have loved old men. I have trusted them, and they have been good to me.

Long ago when I was a boyish schoolmaster in west Cavan, the locals in the pub told me that there was a poet in the old house on the hill.

'He arrived last night,' they said. 'Nobody knows from where or for why.'

They thought it was my duty as the schoolmaster to approach the big old house on the hill and welcome the poet on behalf of the community – me being what they called an 'educated person'. So up I drove that evening, in my Austin A40, and knocked on the door, though it was already open. A second time I knocked without success, but at the third knock I heard a faint voice from within.

'Help!' the poet cried. 'Help!'

263

It was my first encounter with Tom MacIntyre. He had the flu, and over the next few days I fed him rum and fish until he recovered.

I, on the other hand, never recovered. Up to that point in life, I had been a teacher, drinking in local pubs, sitting on the bar stool, staring at my own image in the mirror, until the drink kicked in and the mountain men in damp clothes who smelled of sheep dip seemed like the best company in the world. Then I'd go home and throw myself on a bed that was in the same condition as when I had dragged myself out of it that morning.

MacIntyre's poetic presence caused quite a stir in the parish, and quite a commotion in my soul. All the time he remained in bed – and I remained at the door – he lectured me about life. I was twenty-three. His message was as expected. Carpe diem!

I tried to explain to him that my life was dull; that it was the thing from which I most wanted to escape. I was alienated without understanding why. MacIntyre brought clarity to the subject.

'Clearly,' he declared one evening, 'your current life and career is a place where you don't belong.'

And indeed it proved true. Some years afterwards, I began life again as a writer, and through the years we remained friends. I sought his company in troubled times, and sat by the flickering embers of many fires with him drinking wine. He gave me a tree one time, a bay tree, which still grows so full in Leitrim that we call it the 'MacIntyre Tree', though we have to take a saw to it each year to keep it in check. I have seen him sometimes at Lough Sheelin's shore in the ghostly twilight, out beneath the beech trees among the horses, gathering kindling for his evening fire, like a monk intense in his prayerful ritual, or at early morning picking blackberries, with the enthusiasm of a child.

Not that it's easy sitting with Tom MacIntyre. He doesn't bother with small talk. Like an ancient philosopher, he interrogates his company, usually with variations of the one question – 'What are you doing with your life?' And he can sit for ages without speaking; just sifting the silence for the invisible movements of the mind, like a fisherman waiting for a trout to hop out of a lake. And he knows a lot about lakes.

'Where are you now?' he asked me one time.

'Westmeath,' I said.

'Ah,' he said, 'I presume the "green peter" is hopping on Lough Lane these nights.'

I said, 'I don't know what you're talking about.'

He explained that the green peter is larva that floats up to the surface of lakes in Westmeath in the evenings, during the summer, and hatches on the surface.

'You can see the little flies shake their wings dry and scuttle across the surface. And the trout go mad for them; though there's not many trout left,' he concluded, and he fell silent.

265

On his eightieth birthday he said to me, 'I remember as a child dreaming of two horses, a brown and a dove-grey. It was my first great dream, and now recently I see them again. They return in old age, though not so much the brown, but more frequently the dove-grey.'

MacIntyre traipsed the world from New York to Moscow with his plays and poems. *The Great Hunger* was a ground-breaking play in Irish theatre. *Rise Up, Lovely Sweeney* was unequalled as a meditation on the allure of violence that overrides even eroticism in the Irish psyche. But, most of all, his love songs and translations of love songs, his attachment to all the haunted lakes of Cavan, and his relish for words and all their juicy innuendoes mark him out as an unruly bard in that great tradition of south Ulster poets that reaches back to people like Cathal Buí Mac Giolla Gunna, Peadar Ó Doirnín and Séamas Dall Mac Cuarta.

His conversation is always peppered with references to ghosts and other invisible things, and when he gives poetry readings, the creaking room of shadows wraps itself around him and gives substance to the insubstantial – though speaking of ghosts in a secular age is no way of making yourself fashionable. Fashion never bothered MacIntyre, nor indeed the people who live in those dark drumlins and along the shoreline of Cavan's haunted lakes.

In my opinion, his poetry always proclaimed love to be worth the risk; the extra step certain to transport us to unknown places and bring us out of ourselves. In his storytelling, love always drives the train, upsets the apple carts, is always mischievous and knows no other law but to walk over the cliff blindfolded.

And the wonderful thing about Ireland is that, despite the Famine, the weather, the clergy and the banks, we still possess the brazen optimism to engage with each other, to mind each other and hope for love around the next corner.

'There was this trapdoor,' MacIntyre once wrote, 'at one end of the loft. And nothing would do me but find it –

266

even if I didn't know I was searching for it … I rambled my way to it – the foxglove looking at me, the clover smelling, the daisies basking, the buttercups shiny – and the trap door somehow not fastened – I'm gone, fifteen-foot drop to the stable below. A lap of hay was all that saved me. It wasn't, they said, supposed to be there – but it was. And when people ask me what I believe in, I invariably say – a lap of hay.'

It's not just that in the Rinpoche I had found another MacIntyre, another old man or another father. The crucial fact was that the wind had blown me to the ends of the earth. I was in Mongolia, and felt I was falling through the floor of the world. I was in free fall beyond the trapdoor, but utterly confident and expectant that any moment now I would hit another marvellous lap of hay.

The journey began a few days later. There were nine travellers in all and we had two jeeps – a luxurious Toyota and an old Land Rover, which for some reason people called the Russian jeep. Both vehicles were parked in the courtyard of the monastery one morning and Sukay, a young man with short black hair and denim jeans, was polishing the blue Toyota. And a stout middle-aged man in a white shirt was sitting in the Russian jeep smoking a cigarette. These were our drivers.

At the back of the Russian jeep, Rabsal was fussing about petrol cans and arguing with Bayantsagan, a tall man in a grey suit and grey hair. He was the monastery administrator. A dark-haired girl of about twenty sat in the back of the Toyota dreamily staring out the window at Sukay as he polished the bonnet. Heidi said she was Bayantsagan's niece. And at the door of the Prayer Hall the Rinpoche was in conversation with a young nun.

The nun was going to be our translator. She could interpret from Tibetan to Mongolian. Bayantsagan was on the trip to represent the monastery if anything important happened, and to propagate the name of the monastery as the sponsor of the journey. His niece was there as a companion for the young nun. And the two drivers were there to drive. Rabsal was there to cook noodles for everyone, as he had done for me in India, and Heidi was there because she was a nurse. She would make a report on the health conditions of people we met along the way. Everyone was there because the Rinpoche was there. He was the Panchen Otrul Rinpoche of Tibet. And he was there because the Dalai Lama had asked him to be there. What I was doing there I didn't quite know, apart from the fact that I was a devoted follower of the Rinpoche. But I wasn't inclined to tell anyone that I was having weird erotic dreams and flushes of arousal during my solitary nights in a monastery full of Buddhas.

During the years of Communist domination, many monasteries in Mongolia closed or vanished. The ones that did remain open were restricted in various ways. The

269

teaching of philosophy was curbed. Some old buildings were used for target practice by Soviet tanks on their way to Afghanistan. All monasteries withered in some form or another. Philosophy went into decline. Tens of thousands of monks perished in the Siberian gulags, and a nation of nomadic people were corralled into collective farms they knew nothing about. By the time the Soviet system came to an end, it was nomadic life they knew little about. The monasteries had all vanished and the philosophy which had once been the jewel in the crown of Mongolian civilisation was nothing more than gobbledegook chanted in various huts across the plains by toothless old men who mumbled half-remembered prayers and hadn't a clue what the words meant or what the rituals signified.

So the Dalai Lama arrived in 1991 and promised to send important lamas on visitations, and now here was the Rinpoche in the back of a Toyota jeep ready for the road. I'd had no idea that this frail little man with thick glasses who lived in west Cavan was so important.

We set out on our 2,000-trek with 100-year-old maps of a vast country to seek sites of once-famous monasteries, and to find out what was still standing or what people remembered of long ago centres of learning. We would cross the vast interior of northern Mongolia, where there were no roads or telephones or electricity, and we would wind up our adventure on the shores of a lake near Khovsgol. That was the promise.

In the courtyard, Heidi argued with the monks about the amount of water we were allowed to bring on the journey. Heidi had been there the previous year for a similar expedition with Tibetans and Mongolians, but had become dehydrated. The Tibetans and Mongolians were happy to drink from streams when they needed to, but Heidi knew that the European digestive system would not be as resistant to e-coli bacteria as their Asian bellies. So she was determined that we would take nine litres of water in each jeep to last her and me for two weeks. After she had succeeded in getting the water on board, she came over to me with the nun, Anila, and introduced her, and we sat on the wall and chatted until the rest of the equipment was packed and we were ready to go. Anila's head was bald. She wore round glasses and maroon robes and there wasn't a wrinkle on her young face.

It was almost one in the afternoon before the two jeeps moved out the gates and down the hill and onto the main road and headed west, with two drivers, two women, two monks, one administrator and two Europeans. In the Toyota, Bayantsagan's niece leaned out the window, her long black hair flowing behind her and her white teeth flashing a great smile at all the people on the street and beside the gate who threw cups of milk in the air as we passed through to wish us luck.

The Russian jeep had bad suspension. I couldn't put my feet on the ground because of the drums of gasoline that were stacked on the floor. My knees were in my mouth. My back ached. And then we left the main road and took a track into the grassy plains that led to the mountains. We drove for three hours. The mountains lay before us, soft slopes like sand dunes. Occasionally we saw a few clusters of white dots on the slopes. 'Those are tents,' the driver said. As we came closer, we could see horses and cattle grazing beside the white tents, or yurts as they called them.

As the daylight faded from the sky, we came to a settlement of five or six yurts. The men and women had already assembled outside because they could hear our engines from far off. They brought us inside and offered us bowls of mare's milk, cheese and bread. I could smell cow dung everywhere as we huddled around a fire in the centre of the yurt, eating and chatting, and, when we were leaving, the woman got a ladle and threw milk on the back of the jeeps as we moved out into the dark night.

272   I hoped we would find monks waiting for us somewhere with dry beds and warm food. But we didn't. We just kept driving, hour after hour. It rained. And the landscape resembled an Irish bog. The jeeps went up and down and the headlights sometimes beamed vertically into the black sky. Six hours later we stopped in the middle of nowhere and erected small two-berth tents with uprights and crossbars. The men wrapped me in two pairs of trousers and pushed me into a sleeping bag and then bound the bag with rugs around my feet. I couldn't move. Only my nose

was sticking out when they were finished and it crossed my mind that if I wanted to pee in the night I was in a difficult situation.

'We are high up,' Rabsal explained. 'You must keep warm.'

Thus I was bundled like a mummy into a tent and the driver and administrator got in behind me so that the three of us were mouth to neck like spoons in a drawer. But I slept almost immediately and woke only once. It was so cold that my nose was red and numb. I peeped out through a slit in the canvas. The rain had stopped and the stars were out and, in the distance, I could hear wolves howling.

The following morning, we ate noodles and meat from a pot which Rabsal had cooked the night before. Salami and fresh bread. Each person had a plastic bowl. I saw a single horseman in the distance rounding up his cattle. I saw the nun, Anila, eating from a black wooden bowl unlike anyone else's. I was cold, and when I shivered, Rabsal saw it immediately and came over with his maroon anorak.

We drove all day, stopping for breaks to eat lumps of cheese and bread. In the evening, we ate with another family in a yurt. They gave us cream from a bucket that they kept beneath a bed and the ritual bowls of mare's milk. The Rinpoche gave them pictures of the Buddha, and little red strings and medals with the image of the Dalai Lama.

After three days, we arrived at a derelict monastery, an acre of rubble from the seventeenth century. The main

Prayer Hall was enormous and still intact, a grand dark space of garish images and pungent smells, but the only monks inside were a dozen little boys and they sat with their hands joined in reverence as the Rinpoche walked among them. They performed their prayers for him and then they got curry. Each boy placed his bowl on the low red bench at which they were seated in a line and the senior monk, a teenager in a brown overcoat, came with a bucket of curry and slopped a ladle of it into each bowl. Then he vanished into the kitchen and returned a few moments later with a crate of Coca-Cola. The children were amazed as each one got a bottle and a straw.

Then we were all escorted to a nearby yurt where an old lama lived with his wife. The ancient patriarch was white-haired and he greeted the Rinpoche with great enthusiasm, and cried as if he were meeting an old cousin after many years. His wife, who also had snow-white hair, offered everyone more cheese and more mare's milk. The old teacher was eighty-four and he remembered the time before the Soviets. He looked at Heidi and me and laughed quietly to himself. The Rinpoche exchanged snuff bottles with him. Each man examined the other's bottle and took a tiny spoon of it in the nose and expressed great satisfaction with the other man's gear.

The days developed a pattern. We would drive for hours after breakfast and then stop around noon at whatever settlement we happened to come across. And in these

274

clusters of small tents, we were fed, and the Rinpoche spoke to the family about the Buddha and then we left and drove again into the evening. At each stop, we got more directions for the next part of our journey. Each evening, we set up tents, while Rabsal cooked food for supper and for the following day's breakfast, and then we all rested.

One day we made an unexpected stop in the afternoon at a river. A group of men with horses were resting on the grass bank. The cuckoo was calling in the trees. Rabsal ran off into the fields and returned with a bunch of flowers, which he offered me with both hands outstretched. Anila, the nun, and her girlfriend watched from a distance. They never left the proximity of the Toyota. They stared at me all day but kept as safe a distance as you might from a wild animal. We made a picnic on the riverbank. The girls washed and bathed. When they were finished, I went down to a turn of the river and took off all my clothes and walked into the icy water until I was up to my chest, and the cool sensation of the water on my body was pure bliss.

It was a wonderful picnic. We ate seaweed and rice. Meat and tomatoes. Muesli with chocolate ice-cream. And I clutched Rabsal's wild flowers on my lap. We washed the dishes by rubbing them with dry, dusty earth. The Rinpoche stood over us as we cleaned the vessels.

Eventually, timelessness kicked in. And obedience. And I fell into this obedience as naturally as diving into a lake. I began to accept the world as a child accepts it. I threw

275

stones at a Diet Coke tin. I watched old grandmothers appear out of nowhere with yellow silk scarves to honour the Rinpoche as if he were their long-lost father, and I accepted it all. I had forgotten where I'd come from and I certainly no longer asked myself why I had come. There was no answer.

I had lost my sense of urgency. I had lost my adulthood. I had lost my purpose and my seriousness and my sense that time is important and is measured by clocks. Together with Heidi and the nun and the girl and the monks, I belonged to a family now, with the Rinpoche at the centre. And as long as he wasn't worried about anything, why should I be worried?

And then, one morning, we crossed a high ridge and there before us was the dark pearl of Mongolia, the beautiful lake. So frozen in winter that great trucks could use it as a highway on their way to Russia. Even in summer, there was snow on the far mountains. There were larch trees around the edges and the stones on the shore were white.

We ran to it like children released on a beach. The nun and the girl played in the lapping water. Rabsal took photographs of them and chased them with a mug of water. The girl with black hair and white teeth and skin like almonds took off her green jogging trousers and threw away her light-brown cashmere cardigan and, wearing just her slip and briefs, she jumped up and down in the ice-cool waters and screamed with delight.

I was heartbroken by the sound of her laughter. I felt like I was watching it all from behind a wall of glass. The nun fingering her necklace. The vast waters of the lake. The flat landscape. The larch trees tall and the light through them and the earth dappled beneath them. The trunks of old dead trees bleached white, lying by the water's edge. Stones in the clear water. The nun taking my photograph. Me standing beside her girlfriend who was still half-naked and wet from the lake. The nun giving me the camera and then me taking a picture of them. Both of them standing on a dead log with their arms around each other. The boy falling in love with the girl, and taking every opportunity he could find to be alone with her.

He wore black shoes. She wore white runners. The nun had wooden clogs. I know because I looked at their feet a lot.

In the evening, the administrator stood like a scarecrow by the lakeshore, with rosary beads in each hand. A tall elegant figure in black boots and a grey coat tied at the waist with a yellow scarf. The nun perched on the rocks by the water's edge, her hand in the water playing with the ripples.

And then I slept.

On the second evening by the lakeshore, a family of singers arrived at our camp and put on traditional costumes and played stringed instruments and sang from their throats very sad songs. The star of their show was a young girl, a student from the college of music in Ulaanbaatar, who was on holidays visiting her family. She wore a long red coat with delicate lotus flowers embroidered with golden threads on the sleeves and back that fitted tight to her figure. Her face was a painted mask from the opera and her dark hair was entwined into a ceremonial hat. She took my breath away. She covered the tent with her song as the hush of love and longing overwhelmed me.

The following morning, deep in the woods, I was walking when I thought I saw her again, in costume, standing on a rock in the water a few feet from the shoreline. I went down to say hello and express my gratitude for her singing the previous evening. But as I came close, I realised it was not her. Anila the nun was indulging in a private moment, fully costumed and made up as a princess in the opera.

Our eyes met, and I told her she looked beautiful. She bowed her head and said nothing and I walked on. Farther along the path, I came across her maroon robe, her tights and all her private clothes. And the little compact mirror and pencils and brushes for painting her face.

After that, I felt closer to her. Through each new day, the lines which define one individual as different from another were dissolving. There was no way to use the word 'I' anymore. 'I' didn't function or make sense. 'I' was not human. There was only 'us'. And we were all the same underneath our clothes.

I brought the nun coffee sometimes as we all sat by the campfire at night, and the Rinpoche and Bayantsagan

278

usually talked English, about how many stars above them and how many teas in China and how many small monasteries in Ulaanbaatar and how many monks here and how many monks there; a game of numbers, a way to penetrate the meaning of things.

The Rinpoche came to me one morning and asked if I would cut his fingernails. I said yes. I got the scissors and held his hand. It was fragile and warm, like a bird. And I was thinking of my father's hand resting on the starched linen of his hospital bed many years earlier.

This is the day he will find the monastery he is looking for! I thought. It was just a feeling I had. An instinct. A sense of music in the earth and the sky and the lake that I could hear, and read in his hand, like a signpost. And he did. He found it not far from the lake.

The monastery was a galvanised shed, in the middle of nowhere, and a seventeen-year-old boy in saffron robes welcomed us and lined up seven younger boys in Wellingtons and tattered maroon robes. This was what we had travelled across half of Mongolia to find.

Their mothers stood at the back of the galvanised shed, anxious countrywomen with bright blue and yellow ribbons in their hair and traditional Mongolian coats. Felt boots. Weather-beaten faces. And the wind shook the galvanised roof and rattled the loose doors. The seven young boys were ordained, binding them to certain commitments. They promised to take refuge in the dharma, the wisdom

279

of the Buddha. But, in fact, it was merely a ceremony that gave dignity to their schooling. It committed them to learning the alphabet. To reading and writing. They would be scholar monks from this day forward.

A very important part of the ceremony was when they were vested in yellow robes. But they had only one yellow robe between them so they had to pass it from shoulder to shoulder during the ceremony. At one stage, they all huddled beneath it while the prayers were chanted. They looked silly, squatting like chickens beneath a yellow cloth. But no more silly than I looked when I prostrated myself on the altar of Cavan Cathedral to accept Christian ordination. No more silly than a couple of newlyweds reciting their wedding vows with trembling hands. No more silly than anyone in fear, afflicted by anxiety, who reaches out and takes refuge in something or someone, and asks for help or deliverance from the abyss.

280 All of a sudden, I realised why I had come. And why I had clung to religion for so many years.

It was fear. And it *is* fear. It is always fear. The dread inside that some disaster might befall me if I do not cling to something. The fear of death that lies at the root of all depression. And now maybe I was waking up. I was no longer a believer in anything. I was a writer. I was witnessing something and I would tell the tale.

It was a poor village. They had nothing. Their animals were starving. The coming winter would bring famine.

Entire families would lie with yaks and horses and die in the snow. Perhaps these same boy-monks, whose unlimited hope we were sharing, would not last the winter. Already there was little to eat. In the tent after the ceremony, we had a thin noodle soup without meat. The seven little monks stood around the door, wolfing down lumps of bread. They were shy of the great lama. The breeze was blowing into a gale.

In the distance, I saw a woman walking towards us. Because of the wind and sand, she was sometimes invisible, as the wind blew dust and sand in a swirl around her. She wore a long blue skirt and carried a bucket of yoghurt with one hand and a cloth of cheese curds over her shoulder with the other. When the boys at the door saw her, they were amazed. A banquet was coming. They were in paradise.

Later that day we folded up the tents and the sleeping bags and took a last look at the lake. The jeeps were humming, but before I got in I took a moment alone at the water's edge and promised myself I would return some day.

Part Four

In the moment

On the morning after I died in the movie, I checked out of the Wilton Hotel in Bray and took the DART into Dublin where I paid a visit to my therapist. To conduct her business, she had a long room on the third floor of a city building. There was a couch, two armchairs and a heavy curtain across the door so that the sound of weeping patients didn't travel to the corridor or reception area, and there was an open window through which came the ordinary sounds of life on the street.

My therapist works with the body, and the memories that are contained within the body. She used breathing techniques, to bring the body back to prelingual moments, and to allow sensations from early childhood to surface through the skin. And because I am a writer and impose words on all experience, and constantly reinvent the past in stories, her method was particularly challenging for me. It forced me to close off the verbal narrative in my head. To breathe, and to 'be' in my body, and fall back into the past remembering all the traumas and stresses of my life and of my childhood, and especially of my birth.

I had done about seven sessions with her to prepare, and this session was to be the most important one. I lay on a couch and began to breathe and with her direction floated back to the beginning. Within an hour, the sudden and wonderful moment of birth began again to echo in my skin. I was breathing in and out rapidly, taking deep gulps of air, and I could imagine my mother's slender body above me as I parted from her all those years before.

My birth was so abrupt that the little baby in me was shocked and distressed. And as I lay on the therapist's couch, panting and babbling, those same emotions rose again to the surface. The same shock and distress of my initial entry into the world returned. Myself and my mother had remained in an emotional standoff for the fifty-eight years since, neither of us trusting the other after the sudden parturition, but here I was again back at the beginning. It seemed such a short journey.

I was born at about 2.20 p.m., early in August 1953, in a bedroom of a semi-detached house on Farnham Road in Cavan, but no eagles landed on the gateposts and no thunder was heard in the sky. My father, who had not dreamed of any wondrous portents the night before, went to work as usual and came home for his dinner and then went back to work. He had just arrived back to the accounts department of the county council offices at the back of the courthouse in Cavan Town when one of his colleagues, a tall young man who later became a poet, said, 'You better go home immediately sir, there's been a phone call.'

In those days, phone calls were alarming events. People phoned each other when someone died – or was born. So back he went to Farnham Road, and I presume he took the rest of the day off, but I'm not quite certain. I know nothing about the following few hours.

I can only guess that my mother brought me into the world suddenly and with an alarming abruptness, since it was she who had boiled the potatoes and cooked the chops for my father a few hours earlier, served it all up to him at 1 p.m., and smiled at him later that afternoon in the bed upstairs when he returned from the office. Where I was at that stage I'm not sure. Certainly not on my mother's breast, for she was deeply disappointed that she had not delivered a little girl, and after a few hours she handed me

287

over to Mrs Jenkins, or whoever had been engaged to assist her with the nursing and bathing of the newborn.

It was my mother's second delivery in eighteen months, and she needed some assistance since my father couldn't boil an egg to fend off starvation, let alone fathom the mysteries of washing nappies.

Rebirthing was like recalling a desperate physical struggle. My legs were kicking. I had a pain in my throat, deep down, as if an unpleasant liquid was rinsing my stomach, and I sensed a sudden and frightful fall, downwards into an abyss, which I presume was the light of day.

I cried and screamed for hours after my birth and some would say that I've been crying ever since. When I was an infant, the entire family went on holiday to Enniscrone, a long, flat beach with blue waves and a cluster of bed and breakfast houses on the edge of the town. I was three and my brother was four, and my mother hoped she could cope with both of us plus her husband, but I screamed so loud and so long that before the end of one week, the family had to abandon the holiday and return to Cavan. I even screamed all the way home in the small Austin A7, and when I was brought in the front door of the house on Farnham Road, I stopped.

As a boy, I spent my leisure time climbing trees, catching bees and eventually, when I was old enough to cycle five miles out the road, I walked by the shoreline of various lakes. In Cavan there was a tapestry of lakes, linked by the

River Erne, which meandered through the county and around the drumlins, leaving beautiful pools of water in every hollow.

'Where *were* you?' my mother would ask as I came for tea on a summer's evening.

'Out at the lake,' I would reply.

No one ever asked what I was doing out there. No one questioned me. It was the most natural thing in the world to be drawn to lakes. Some people throw themselves in lakes and, occasionally in Cavan, a person would disappear and the neighbours would whisper that the police were dragging the lake. But lakes never attracted me like that. I may have been sad, but I trusted the universe. Lakes were places where the pike lived among the reeds, where the water hens called, where the swans mooched about with their young, where the fly swarmed in May and the moon reflected on autumn evenings.

I missed my mother from the moment I was suddenly ejected, and she looked at me disappointedly and wished I was a girl, but I trusted the universe. And the lakes were safe.

I knew a professor in later life who walked into a lake, and was dragged out a few days later with his fist still locked around his briefcase. I guessed his briefcase was his worry blanket and the lake was his mother, or what he hoped was his mother, enveloping him in tenderness for just once in his life. But I knew the lake was not my mother. My mother was a slim woman in a frock who made almond buns and apple dumplings. Lakes were just spaces filled with water, but that was enough to astonish me because depression is about the mind shrinking to a tiny size, but when we look at a lake, our mind expands. Not with ideas, but simply with the size of the lake.

And then there were trees. My mother often left me in a pram at the end of the garden because I wouldn't stop crying and, eventually, the shimmering of a thousand green leaves became for me a calming presence around the pram. Ever since, I have retained a sense of the nurturing and maternal power of woodlands. As I sat recovering, I would observe that trees often remind me of my Auntie Molly, all blousy and heavy-breasted. But they also have a way of opening up the universe. In their sculpture and structure, in their leaf and light and especially the complex movement of the wind in their branches, trees open to me a space that fills with consciousness and wakens in me a sense of belonging.

I know lots of people who have been angry with their mothers for decades, feeling that they didn't get all the love that was their due as infants or children. Perhaps I was lucky because my mother gave me everything. She fed me and clothed me and lit a thousand candles in various churches for my well-being. She may not have hugged me very much, but she gave me buns and apple tarts. And beyond that, I found a deeper mother in the world and in all its loveliness. And beyond God, I found a lake, nothing more and nothing less; that quiet shoreline where I still walk to quench the undying embers of anger and rage.

After the therapy session, I could barely walk down the street. The therapist had advised me to go and eat something, so I had lunch in Boyers of North Earl Street. The stew was only €8.50 and I had a coffee and bread pudding as well for just €2 extra. The seating area was full of elderly ladies with grey hair and old men with shopping bags.

I like Boyers. I am drawn to its cosy café because I often met my mother there, years ago, when she would come up on the bus from Cavan after her husband died and she got the free travel pass. But when I visit her now in the nursing home, she's always asleep, and there's not much talking can be done, and it is unlikely that she will ever be able to come to Boyers again to look at the clothes, like she loved doing, even in her seventies.

The day I was reborn on the therapist's couch, my mother was still in the nursing home in Westmeath, not far from Lough Ennell, where she once cycled as a girl to meet apple-picking boys, when she was on her summer holidays in her grandfather's pub in Castlepollard.

There was something heroic about her solitude in sleep, because she was the last of eight children who all used to go on holidays to Westmeath. A train took them from Cavan station, and a pony and trap completed the journey from Inny Junction to the square in Castlepollard. She was the last of her siblings. I suppose the others still existed in her dreams and memory. I imagined them all running around the station, mad with excitement waiting for the train. I imagined Freddy, the little chubby red-haired boy who would sing 'Mother Machree' at parties, and Oliver, the nervous altar boy, and Johnny, the shy ghost at everyone's table, and Paddy, the one who never got his fair share of any cake.

But they're all gone. And still my mother sleeps and holds them in her memory. I imagined her sister Bernadette, a young, slender girl with a passion for fashionable hats, as nervous as a fawn and deaf in one ear. And Molly the brash stout girl who bossed the others, played the piano and instructed the younger ones in their lessons. And Nancy, a wiry slip of a tomboy who smoked cigarettes behind the wall of Halpin's orchard. Eight of them at the wooden board where their father would sit in boots full of money, when he had returned with pigs from Belfast for the factory in Cavan, and when fresh parsley floated on her mother's chicken soup on the black range in the kitchen of their home.

But everything is gone now: the pony and trap, the railway station, Halpin's apple trees, and all the children who sat around that kitchen table. And yet my mother lasts and sleeps, alone, and holds it together in her heart. All you have to do sometimes is hold her hand and say, 'Mother, do you remember the Bridge of Finea?' and she will smile and squeeze your hand, and say, 'There's money under that bridge.'

Eventually it will all dissolve, I suppose, the fabric of life that they wove together. The arguments and jealousies, the excitement over frocks and weddings and childbirths and graduations and then more weddings when she and her sisters became the aunties with the funny hats.

I remember all the funerals, one after another, and my mother standing at each open coffin and scrutinising the faces of her siblings. But still she endures, quietly breathing, her eyes opening now and again for a cup of water or a bite of an Aero bar, as she smiles at the nurses.

'Will you say a prayer for me, Nellie?' the nurse said one day. And Nellie nodded because that was her name. That's what she was called when her father drove the pony and trap to the station to wait for the train, and the long hot summer stretched before them all. The fields and meadows around Lough Ennell, white with daisies and loud with corncrakes and honeybees and apple-picking boys. There they waited, in the stillness of a railway station. And though she is limp now and dry-lipped, and lies all day in a bed with cot sides and a drip sending tiny drops of sustenance through her bony arm, I prefer to imagine her at the station in her grandfather's pony and trap, quietly excited in a summer frock, and just waiting for summer to begin.

Such were my feelings as I returned to Leitrim after my meditations in the coffin and my rebirthing on a therapist's couch. I was thinking of something John Moriarty used to

293

say – 'We all need a cradle to be born in and we all need a cradle to die in.' I had seen both in the space of forty-eight hours. The coffin to die in and the wide world where my mother allowed me to be cradled by some invisible hand. But I was also thinking how strange it was that my mother should appear so beautiful and young and slender, and in a frock.

No wonder I spent hours as a child rummaging in her closet when she was out of the house, putting on dresses and walking in her shoes and powdering myself with her powder puffs, until I finally found the linen and lace of a priestly vocation.

When she was out of the house, I used to steal upstairs to where the Child of Prague stood on a dressing table with his arms outstretched. He stood on a lace mat and on either side of him were dainty little silver boxes. One was for my mother's necklaces and bracelets and the other was full of powder for making up her face. I had all I required there to impress the Almighty in a ritual and gobbledegook that closely resembled the local parish priest mumbling his Latin. It was my first experiment in the hocus pocus abracadabra world of wonder. The first time I tried to make the invisible visible by the performance of a ritual.

I remember once saying mass in Nôtre Dame in Paris. It was a weekday and I was permitted to celebrate mass on a side-altar. The sacristan unlocked the gates of the enclosed alcove. I entered, and then he locked me in. I didn't realise that people were watching me through the bars of the grille or that to enact the Eucharistic rite was as exotic to Japanese tourists as a samurai ritual from the Middle Ages. But when I elevated the consecrated bread in the air above my head in what I thought was a private moment between me and the Almighty God, I was stunned by what sounded like a flock of pigeons flapping their wings. When I turned around I was blinded by a battery of cameras discharging their flashes, as dozens of tourists captured the experience to bring it home with them. For me, it was a terrifying moment; the secular world was rattling my cage. But at the altar I had complete refuge. I surrendered to the ancient stones of the great cathedral and to the silver chalice and to the isolation of public ritual and most especially to the warm glow which I believed at the time was the tenderness of my heavenly mother enveloping me.

So on the day after I died, and on the evening of my rebirth, I returned to Leitrim by train, dreaming of Mother even as the train swept through Mullingar, where my real mother was sleeping in a nursing home. I got off at Carrick-on-Shannon and drove home to the mountain. I went out to the green galvanised shed in the garden and made a decision. It was time to build something new – a workspace or perhaps even a new studio – a place where I could begin again.

I missed my daughter, and some days I couldn't get her out of my head. She had gone to college. She was living her own life now, no longer under the shelter of her parents. But the cottage in Leitrim still resonated with the remnants of her childhood, which seemed eternal when we were in the middle of it and yet it had passed like leaves falling off a tree, suddenly and unexpected.

In the shed behind the house, I would sometimes stand when it was raining and think about her. A green galvanised shed that had stood there for years. It was painted green by three wise young men who came out of the blue one summer day in a white van and said they possessed the best paint in the universe. Paint that was used by Harland and Wolff to paint ships. Paint that would never peel in an aeon of Leitrim winters. In fact, the paint was peeling off by the end of the following November but nobody complained. The shed was only used for storing things. Plastic bags of furry toys. Old furniture. The books and CDs and broken radios that got edged out of life as we moved along with new fashions. There were even a few bits of the bed I was born in leaning against the wall. And a hammer we lost years ago. A high-heeled shoe enfolded in light cobweb lay on the window-sill. There was a picture of Harry Houdini. An old pot-bellied stove. And the tea chest where the cat had had her kittens sixteen years earlier, which had ended in tragedy. A one-eyed white tomcat from down the road attacked one night and left the kittens strewn around the yard like small wet gloves in the rain.

One day in spring, I decided to visit my daughter in Galway. Just for a quick lunch, I said in a text. And I said 1 p.m. I stressed 1 p.m in a second text. I suppose I was always a man who fretted about lunch dates, especially with important people. And there wasn't anyone more important than Sophia.

We planned to meet on Quay Street, outside McDonagh's fish and chip restaurant, and coming up to 1 p.m., I was reading the menu and composing fairytales with happy endings in my head to keep myself relaxed.

But everything reminded me of the past. Near the AIB Bank, a performance artist in monochrome silver was replicating the statue of Pádraic Ó Conaire which had once stood in Eyre Square, and this reminded me of the first time I had seen the real statue, when I was ten years old. And Ó Conaire, a wild and passionate man, who died before he was fifty, reminded me of friends who also died too young; an artist, Pat Bracken, who used to drink in The Bunch of Grapes, and Bernard Galligan, an old school mate who used to sell oysters at the top of Mainguard Street, and John O'Donohue, who used to pore over the books in Kenny's bookshop.

John O'Donohue, the philosopher from west Clare who had been in my class in college and who had journeyed with me to Italy in a truck, all those years ago. John who had laughed and joked all the way over the top of the Alps, and who had insisted we stop at the very top of the mountain when he'd spied an old church in the fog and snow. A caretaker had brought us inside, and we saw a splendid altar, on which stood two majestic candlesticks. The caretaker had said that Napoleon had come across the snowy path on one occasion and had rested there and had sent the candlesticks as a gesture of his gratitude after he had returned to Paris.

I remember John fingering them with love and reverence;

it was the way he touched everything he came in contact with that made my skin tingle with admiration for him – the flowers of the Burren, the rocky fields of Connemara and the hearts of all the people he met around the world, through his writings. He was intensely alive.

I remember him talking to the abbot in the monastery we stayed at in Venice. About Caravaggio, and the sound of his laughter in the refectory when he saw the monks put brandy on their ice-cream at Sunday lunch.

In the years that followed, John and I rarely met, except perhaps by accident; like that one time in the doorway of Kenny's bookshop when we brushed by each other with the aloof courtesies of old friends who have grown apart.

In the autumn of 2007 John was in New York, and I know he went to a concert in the Lincoln Centre where a violinist was playing Tchaikovsky's Concerto in D. He had a single seat near the front. He was so close to the young musician that he could feel the intensity in her body as she played. She was so alive in the passionate and creative act of making music that he'd wept. It was the measure of how intensely John O'Donohue loved life, and how he revered the beauty in other human beings. He told the story to an interviewer from Public Radio in December, but by the time the interview was broadcast the following month, John had been laid to rest in a graveyard in Clare. He had no grey hairs and he was enjoying a wonderful life, but he did not get the chance that old age brings to sit back and

299

relish the past. And that's what I find hard to accept about life; that it passes so swiftly.

In fact, it feels like only yesterday that my own daughter was born in the snow at the end of February 1993. Her tiny wrinkled face sideways on the pillow, as they wheeled her little incubator out of the delivery suite. I couldn't take my eyes off her. And the following morning I walked through the snow-covered streets in search of the cot shop. It was an ordinary day for the shop assistant. She showed me all sorts and sizes of cots. She showed me the cheaper ones, the sensible ones, the practical and the sturdy ones. And she showed me the top of the range, the Rolls Royce of cots.

As I bundled it into the boot of the car, the snow in a foggy swirl of flakes around me, my hands were trembling. I had just bought something for my daughter! The following weeks were peppered with little intensities of love, shared by the three of us. The new parents and the beautiful child. We lived in a bubble of glee, lit by a slanting March sun which lavished its shafts of joyful light in the room where mother and child were recovering and building their strength.

One day I came to the window, and my beloved opened it, letting in draughts of crisp air, and I waited as she covered the baby's head for fear of the chill before passing in fresh daffodils. There were moments in the dead of night when we both leaned over the cot, like two farmers at a gate, listening to the soft breathing of the bundle in the blanket.

300

And there were other nights, when her crying felt like slow torture, and we would take it in turns to pace the floor cooing at her and jogging her, in the hope that she might fall asleep. One night all the nursery tunes I ever heard collapsed, and I ended up chanting a Hare Krishna mantra to her for half an hour.

But she grew up, suddenly and without warning. I had not really noticed her stretch the length of the cot. I had not really noticed the speed with which she slipped from one phase to another; from new teeth to new words, talking and walking, and eating and sitting in cars, and making friends, and going to play school. Fully dressed, she waited at the patio door, her face to the glass, shouting, 'Car!' Her blue plastic lunch box in her hand, her blue beret cocked to the side. On the drive to town, she named her territory. That's the broken house. There's the caravan in the field. The digger digging the road. The donkey on the hill. And in the play school, she tossed her lunch box in my direction and dashed round the corner to the toys.

When I returned, she was breathless. Telling me how 'We painted and we made bird tables and we went down the slide and we played with the teapots.'

On the way home, I stopped at the Pound Store and bought her a Barney balloon, a purple dinosaur on a yellow background in a bubble of helium gas. She was amazed. But still she checked her world. The caravan was in the field. The digger was on the road. The donkeys were in

301

their usual place on the hill. In the kitchen, she sat by the range, her balloon of gas floating above her head. Its string hanging down by the side of her face. She munched a jam sandwich and swilled down her bottle of milk. But bed was out of the question. She would not be put down. She fought exhaustion until the lids fell over her eyes, slowly, completely, and she was asleep, but still upright. The teapots were sleeping. The birds were sleeping. The toys and the caravan and the houses were sleeping. She nodded by the whispering range, the bottle on the floor, the sandwich crusts on her lap, and the string of her Barney balloon gripped tightly in her hand. The yellow globe of helium gas floated above her, like a big ship anchored.

And when she went to Mullingar as a young teenager, she did find enormous fun in stable yards, riding horses and competing in shows. She even had her own pony, a beautiful chestnut gelding called Darwin.

302   Darwin grew up on an organic farm, eating herbs, and he had long brown eyelashes and enormous brown eyes. He had a girlfriend, Gem, a grey mare in the adjoining stable. Each morning, he put his head out to look for her. Each evening, he talked to her through a gap in the wall between the two stables. When they were being put out to the fields, Darwin always wanted Gem beside him. And going to a show, he was only happy if Gem came with him. Otherwise he would kick the walls of the horse box, from Mullingar to Wexford and back again with rage.

Darwin, they said, had a sense of humour. He always flung his feed bucket out over the stable door when he was finished, as a joke. And he would turn his hind rump to the door if someone he didn't like came in. But a stable yard can also be the setting for great tragedies. One day, a man, worrying about his debts, was holding the reins of his daughter's pony and gazing at the sky, as the farrier worked on the horse's feet, when suddenly his heart burst and he fell down dead. On another occasion, a little boy was found crying in the corner of an empty stable because his parents had just announced to him that, on account of financial problems, they had sold his pony. And one of the saddest things in any yard is the sight of a horse not ridden, because the young rider has lost interest, and the lovely beast is left abandoned, unexercised and lonely.

But Darwin was never lonely. For the princess who grew up with donkeys in the hills above Lough Allen, he was a dream come true. He took her over all the fences she ever faced, though it was more than jumping kept them together; she really loved him, and he loved her. He loved to toss his bucket at her. To roll on the ground with her, and blow breath into her face, to stretch for apples, or just chew Silvermints, while she plaited his tail.

She came every day after school, without fail, whether it was wet or fine, and together they learned to jump higher and higher over the fences. He jumped so well that, within the first year of their relationship, he had chalked up over

303

two hundred points, for clear rounds at various shows. And as a Grade A pony, he went on to win so many leagues and competitions that he became fussy about photographs, and often refused to stand beside other horses he didn't like when the photographer came to capture his image for the local newspaper. And when she grew too big for ponies, she knew that she must sell Darwin so that he could continue his adventures with some other princess. For a few days, everyone in the yard was silent. The young girl hugged him and played with him, and told him how much she would miss him. She rode him bareback to be close to him, and played her usual games with him. And then, one morning in May, the lorry arrived. The young girl handed the driver apples, to give to Darwin at various times on the long journey to comfort him.

The lorry driver was a kind man and he listened carefully to her, and reassured her about everything. People stood around in tears, broken-hearted, afraid to look each other in the eye. But the young girl was brave, and she did look Darwin in the eye, one last time, as the ramp was lifted and locked, and she smiled, so that he wouldn't think she was upset.

That evening Darwin crossed the Irish Sea, and travelled as far as Devon where he spent a night. Then he and the driver crossed to Calais, and on through Europe, as far as Denmark. Finally they arrived in Sweden, by ferry, to meet a new princess. And on that May morning, as the lorry drove off down the lane beneath the green beeches, everyone headed up the yard again, with wheelbarrows and forks because there were other horses to feed. Life had moved on and what happened to the princess after that moment is her own story, and I will leave it for her to tell someday in the future.

Every young person in the city reminded me of my princess, each with their own secret joy, as they wandered in and out of the shops and talked on mobiles. And then I looked at my watch and realised it was almost 2 p.m. and the waitress was getting impatient because I was a long time sitting and had ordered nothing. So I told her I wasn't hungry anymore, and I left €2 on the table and walked back up the street, dejected at being stood up, until a voice bellowed at me from a table just outside Fat Freddy's.

'Dad,' the voice called out. 'Where were you? I've been waiting here for the past hour.'

And I saw her sitting there, with her Canon camera and her café latte; a young woman, ready and waiting.

While was writing this book of stories and remembrance, the green shed was dismantled and taken away and half a dozen men worked outside behind the house building a new studio, with a blazing bonfire on site to keep the midges away. A room twenty feet by sixteen feet, with a stove and chimney on the north wall, a window on the south wall, an apex ceiling with two skylights, and a six-foot-wide patio door looking out on Lough Allen and the slopes of Sliabh an Iarainn.

The new building seemed to appear out of nowhere.

Day by day the blocks rose from a cement foundation, and the windows were put in and the crossbeams and planks cut and shaped for the roof and finally the slates went on. They were black and glistened in the rain. It was a great team of workers. The plasterer was from Arigna, and the block layer from Limerick, and a man from Drumshanbo, who spent years roofing buildings in New York, put the slates on. They hammered and plastered and blocked away every day from 7 a.m. until 6 p.m. and even though I was excited to see the building take shape, I stayed away from the site while the workers were there. But in the evenings when they had all finished and drove away in a red van, I would sometimes stand in the shell of it to examine the view from what would soon be my patio door, and wonder about the future.

Who knows what the future will be like? Perhaps our children will live in houses where open fires are illegal. Perhaps the image of Santa sitting at the fireside will be airbrushed out, just like the crib was erased from all our Christmas cards. Perhaps a brave new world is coming where people will accept that life ends in the grave and that heaven is a poppycock of the unconscious mind. Perhaps the next generation will concoct a world where belief in the child of Bethlehem is seen as the crude remnant of a mediaeval imagination, unsustainable in a secular, sophisticated Europe of rational human beings.

I don't know.

But it's a long time since I stayed up all night in the chapel in Maynooth, getting high on incense and whispered prayers, as I abandoned myself into the arms of Jesus, hour after hour before the white altar, during an all-night vigil for peace in the week before Christmas. All the hymns were strong anthems of masculinity and the sleeping boys around me looked like cherubs, fresh-skinned and almond-eyed, though I'm not sure how many of them ever found peace. I suppose a lot of them are grey-haired clerics now, with pincushioned noses or trembling hands, alone in the stone cold kitchens of crumbling presbyteries.

One Sunday evening in late July 2012, my brother Brendan went to visit my mother, and phoned me from the nursing home where she was sleeping and said he thought she would not last much longer. I drove to Mullingar and checked into the Park Hotel and then went to the nursing home where he was sitting by her bed and she was breathing heavily, her eyes closed, her face sideways on the pillow.

We stayed a few hours and then went away to our hotels for some rest. Brendan returned at 3 a.m. and I at 4 a.m. The following hours were quiet, apart from her breathing which became more rapid as the night wore on. Being a physician, my brother knew she was going, and around 5 a.m., he began touching her in a form of blessing and in a way that seemed to lighten the mood in the room. By 6 a.m., we were both sitting on the bed, holding her, and she took her last few breaths with long spaces between each one until eventually there was no more breath left and the muscles of her face relaxed for the last time into the serene and indifferent mask of death. I could hear a musician playing a concertina in the distance because someone had turned on a radio at the far end of the corridor. Brendan and I sat for a while without speaking. I felt her presence in the room, perhaps closer than at any moment in my life. I wanted to stay there forever but we couldn't, so eventually we went up to the Park Hotel and had breakfast and discussed the funeral.

Later in the morning, the undertaker came from Cavan in a black Transporter van, and I helped him move the remains to a trolley and then discreetly to the van, and I drove behind it all the way to Cavan, along the roads that she had so often travelled before I was born. It was a wet day and people in Cavan Town were going about their ordinary business with umbrellas as we drove through, and nobody would have known that inside the black van were the remains of my mother.

309

On Tuesday, she lay in her coffin and friends came and looked at her and shook our hands and there were many sweet conversations about the past. I kissed her forehead before the lid was closed down on her. The last kiss, I told myself, must last my lifetime.

And on Wednesday, she was buried in Killygarry cemetery, beside her husband, just outside the church where they had been married sixty years earlier.

As she faded in the last hour of her life, it seemed as if her entire identity surfaced on the texture of her skin. I saw a beautiful woman sleeping by the fire, dozing before the television and counting buns on a tray in the kitchen. I saw a young girl dancing in Cork and I saw the old woman who endured thirty years in her front room, looking at television and mostly alone. It all surfaced in the last few moments in the expression on her face. When the final breath had left her, she seemed as empty as a bowl and as cleaned out and pure as a newborn baby. And as the moment arrived, the corridor outside filled with music.

In August, the builders finished my studio. The rafters were put in place, the roof slates fitted, and the floorboards laid. The windows and the patio door were sealed, the walls plastered and rendered and I stood in it for the first time and looked out at the lake and realised I had returned once again to a place of true belonging.

When we abandon all our beliefs and dogmas that are spun in fear and when we release ourselves from anxiety and surrender to the mothering that the earth can do and the healing that time can offer. When we stop worrying about ourselves and trust the wide earth and the deep blue waters to hold us. When we come to the realisation that I cannot be human without you. That's the moment that opened for me at a lake in Mongolia. That's the moment that opened for me when my mother gave me birth and I was thrown out into this anxious world on a one-way ticket. Just as

310

poetry widens our conscious mind, so too the world invites us in, and when we greet the world, a space opens up, into which consciousness flows just as water makes a lake in every hollow.

I write this in Leitrim, on 6 August 2012. In front of me, the mountain is covered with mist and, below me, the lake is like a mirror. I can hear the sound of a chisel on stone from the other end of the garden where Cathy is busy in her studio. I sit at the stove in this new space for the first time and, just for old time's sake, I pour pure water into seven golden water bowls and I light a candle. And I begin all over again.

With thanks:

To Cathy Carman, Brendan Harding, Finbar Coady and Fergal Fox for their love and support.

To Ciara Doorley for her encouragement, guidance and editorial brilliance and to my agent Jonathan Williams for his vigilance regarding the text.

And to Christy, who put up the building, and Vincent, who did the plastering.

Some of the reflections contained in this memoir have previously appeared in Michael Harding's columns in The Irish Times, *and some on* Sunday Miscellany *on RTÉ and on* The Quiet Corner *on Lyric FM.*